The
Popol
Vuh

The
Popol
Vuh

A NEW ENGLISH VERSION

Translated from the K'iche' by

Michael Bazzett

MILKWEED EDITIONS

Published 2018 by Milkweed Editions
Printed in the United States
Cover design and illustration by Mary Austin Speaker
Author photo by Leslie Bazzett
Interior design by Mary Austin Speaker
21 22 23 24 25   7 6 5 4 3
First Edition

Milkweed Editions, an independent nonprofit publisher, gratefully acknowledges sustaining support from the Jerome Foundation; the Lindquist & Vennum Foundation; the McKnight Foundation; the National Endowment for the Arts; the Target Foundation; and other generous contributions from foundations, corporations, and individuals. Also, this activity is made possible by the voters of Minnesota through a Minnesota State Arts Board Operating Support grant, thanks to a legislative appropriation from the arts and cultural heritage fund, and a grant from Wells Fargo. For a full listing of Milkweed Editions supporters, please visit milkweed.org.

Library of Congress Cataloging-in-Publication Data

Names: Bazzett, Michael, author.
Title: The Popol vuh : a new English version / Michael Bazzett.
Other titles: Popol vuh. English
Description: First edition. | Minneapolis, Minnesota : Milkweed Editions, [2018] | Includes bibliographical references.
Identifiers: LCCN 2017050716 (print) | LCCN 2017051732 (ebook) | ISBN 9781571319180 (ebook) | ISBN 9781571314680 (pbk. : alk. paper)
Subjects: LCSH: Popol vuh. | Popol vuh--Poetry. | Quiché mythology.
Classification: LCC F1465.P8 (ebook) | LCC F1465.P8 B3913 2018 (print) | DDC
    299.7/8423--dc23
LC record available at https://lccn.loc.gov/2017050716

Milkweed Editions is committed to ecological stewardship. We strive to align our book production practices with this principle, and to reduce the impact of our operations in the environment. We are a member of the Green Press Initiative, a nonprofit coalition of publishers, manufacturers, and authors working to protect the world's endangered forests and conserve natural resources. *The Popol Vuh* was printed on acid-free 30% postconsumer-waste paper by Thomson-Shore.

Contents

Introduction vii

PART ONE

Preamble   3
The Beginning   6
The Creation of Animals   11
Figures of Mud and Figures of Wood   15
The Flood   22

PART TWO

Seven Macaw   31
The Fall of Seven Macaw   34
The Shooting of Seven Macaw   38
Zipacna and the 400 Boys   46
The Defeat of Zipacna   54
The Defeat of Cabracan   59

PART THREE

The Story of the Father of Hunahpu and Xbalanque   69
The Summons to Xibalba   76
The Descent into Xibalba   81
Lady Blood and the Tree of One Hunahpu   90
The Ascent of Lady Blood from Xibalba   95
Lady Blood and the Miracle of Maize   101
Hunahpu and Xbalanque in the House of Xmucane   107
The Fall of One Batz and One Chouen   116
Hunahpu and Xbalanque in the Maizefield   121
Hunahpu and Xbalanque Discover the Gaming Things 131

The Summons of Hunahpu and Xbalanque to Xibalba   134
The Descent of Hunahpu and Xbalanque into Xibalba   144
Hunahpu and Xbalanque in the House of Cold   164
Hunahpu and Xbalanque in Jaguar House   166
Hunahpu and Xbalanque in the House of Fire   167
Hunahpu and Xbalanque in Bat House   168
The Head of Hunahpu Restored   174
The Death of Hunahpu and Xbalanque   178
The Resurrection of Hunahpu and Xbalanque   184
The Summons of Hunahpu and Xbalanque before the Lords 186
Hunahpu and Xbalanque Dance before the Lords of Xibalba 189
The Defeat of the Lords of Xibalba   194
The Miraculous Maize of Hunahpu and Xbalanque   197
The Sun, Moon, and Stars   204

PART FOUR
The Creation of Humanity   209
The Discovery of Maize   211
The First Four People   215
The Vision of the First Men   216
Gratitude of the First Men   219
The Displeasure of the Gods   222
The First Four Women   225
The Beginnings of the People   227
The First Dawn   235

Notes   241

The Popol Vuh: A Reader's Companion   245

Introduction

Somewhere in a highland cloud forest in the middle 1500s, near the place where the continents of the Americas hinge upon their mountainous spine, a story was written down. The marks were likely made on paper made from bark, with ink darkened by soot. This story was already many centuries old—thousands of years, in fact—and it was etched into the hearts of the scribe or scribes who wrote it. It no doubt tripped readily from their lips in an incantatory rhythm. And it was written down secretly, line by line, the phonetic rendering of a living pulse, and spirited away. So the story goes.

For a century and a half, no outsiders saw this book. Not a whisper of it appears anywhere. Not until the beginning of the eighteenth century, when a Dominican friar named Francisco Ximénez gained the trust of his K'iche' parishioners and access to the manuscript, and copied the original K'iche' text down verbatim.

Ximénez wrote that "it was with great reserve that these manuscripts were kept among them, with such secrecy, that neither the ancient ministers knew of it, and investigating this point, while I was in the parish of Santo Tomas Chichicastenango, I found that it was the doctrine which they first imbibed with their mother's milk, and that all of them knew of it almost by heart, and I found that they had many of these books among them." The secrecy is understandable, given that early Spanish missionaries fed hundreds of Mayan books into the flames of their bonfires in their attempt to eradicate "superstition and the lies of the Devil."

Ximénez's manuscript is faded and stained in places, with no sectional organization, and haphazard punctuation and capitalization. The original unknown author had clearly mastered the Latin alphabet of the Spaniards. The Maya were highly literate, with an alphabet both glyphic and phonetic, and facility with the new characters came easily. But there was no attempt at lineation or other conventions of verse; the pages are filled with monolithic columns of uninterrupted prose—as if a river of poetry had been poured into a bucket.

The original manuscript has never been recovered, and its author remains unknown. In a strange and lovely meta-twist, the disappearance of this K'iche' manuscript, the "lost book" that served as Ximénez's source, is echoed in the very tale it tells. The prologue alludes to the existence of an even earlier ur-text:

The original book exists.
It was written long ago
but those who read and ponder it
have hidden their faces.

We are thus left with the copy of an echo. An echo of a "lost book" that the authors themselves refer to as an *ilb'al*, an instrument of sight. An instrument of divine vision providing a window into the thoughts of the gods. Such is the story of the *Popol Vuh*.

❦

Four hundred years after Ximénez transcribed his manuscript, in the spring of 2009, an archaeology student was peeling roots and earth from a stone structure in the ancient Mayan city of El

Mirador, in northern Guatemala, when he uncovered two stone panels. He was part of a team investigating the water collection systems of El Mirador, and the discovery of the beautifully carved frieze was utterly unexpected. As team leader Richard Hansen put it, "It was like finding the Mona Lisa in the sewage system."

The panels date to 200 BCE, nearly two thousand years before Ximénez put pen to paper. Hansen pointed out that "to find this story in the Preclassic period is beyond belief. For many years it was thought that the *Popol Vuh* creation story had been contaminated by the Spanish priests who translated it—that the Indians had been influenced by Christianity. This frieze shows that the Maya account of creation was vibrantly established for thousands of years before the Spanish got here. It's like finding the original copy of the Constitution. I was stunned."

The frieze illustrates a key moment from the epic, where Hunahpu, one of the mythic hero twins, has discovered the severed head of his father, who battled the lords of death and paid the ultimate price. Hunahpu is accompanied by his brother, Xbalanque, as they swim in a river of the underworld. The panel lines a channel designed to guide rainwater into cisterns. It seems fitting to me that this story would compose the veins of a city, gathering its vital fluid, its *kik'*, to sustain it through the dry seasons.

In the spring of 2009, while the ruins at El Mirador were being excavated, I was researching a new course, thousands of miles to the north. I've found that in a twenty-first-century world so utterly saturated with information, my students crave nothing more than the authentic, and I hoped to tap into that hunger with an exploration of myth. Needless to say, the *Popol Vuh* was high on my list of possible texts. I was intrigued at the prospect of reading it alongside Genesis or the *Odyssey*, yet the only translations I could find were scholarly prose, dense with footnotes. They are fascinating, vivid work to be sure, but not what I hoped to place beside the poetry of Seamus Heaney's *Beowulf* or Stephen Mitchell's *Gilgamesh* in a literature classroom. My students are bright, lively, and curious: I craved a version of the myth they could disappear into, a verse version that truly sang.

This is my attempt to make just such a thing, to breathe life into old words and resuscitate this story for a new audience, with the end goal of creating a lucid poem that the modern reader can enter and disappear into with minimal framing. As Homer put it, I hoped to help the poem "Sing for our time too."

Such a project is not without peril, of course. The Maya believe that ancestors are made to live again when we speak their words—the word they use is *k'astajisaj*, meaning "to endow with life" or "to resurrect." As Allen Christenson relates in the introduction of his excellent translation: "When the words of the ancestors are read, or spoken aloud, it is as if that person had returned from death to speak again. Reading ancient texts is therefore a very delicate matter, filled with peril if the words are not treated with sufficient respect."

I have approached this task with these very words in mind. And I've been a little haunted by the thought of the many hundreds of books burned by zealous missionaries while the Maya looked on with rage, despair, and crushing grief as the flames consumed the voices of their grandparents. I have been guided in my choices as a reader and a poet, and thus this has been a literary endeavor as much as a scholarly one. That said, I have hewed with as much fidelity to the text, and its spirit, as possible. The Ximénez manuscript served as the original source, and every line of the poem has its antecedent in the K'iche'.

Any work of translation must drink deeply of what has come before it, and this version is no exception. I am particularly indebted to Allen Christenson's meticulous and indispensable two-volume translation, which served as the touchstone for this work. The second volume, his "literal" word-for-word translation from the K'iche', served as my trot, the scaffold upon which I was able to build this version. I have also read and learned much from the translations of Dennis Tedlock, Delia Goetz and Adrián Recinos, Munro Edmonson, and Sam Colop (to Spanish). Both Christenson's and Tedlock's notes were invaluable in helping me decipher and interpret many passages, and Christenson's essay on parallelisms and chiastic structures was tremendously useful as I sought to unearth a poetic structure from Ximénez's solid columns of prose.

When read aloud, the rhythm of the *Popol Vuh* is sinuous and propulsive. The preponderance of this version alternates between a loose three-beat and a four-beat line, as this most effectively captures the elastic nature of the telling, and I occasionally attempt to highlight its momentum through enjambment. To help echo the cadences of spoken K'iche', with its husky consonants spoken deep in the throat and its marvelous sinewy music, I favored Anglo-Saxon roots over the Latin whenever possible, for their consonantal husk and immediacy, as well as their ability to signify a certain rootedness. When the K'iche' verb has a particular resonance, difficult to capture in English, I attempt to bring that to light via metaphor. For instance, finding no equivalent for *pupuje'ik* (which Domingo de Basseta defined in his *Vocabulario de lengua quiche* as "the way in which clouds rise up from the mountains"), I use an image to bring flavor to the verb:

To make earth they said, "Earth"

and there it was: sudden
as a cloud or a mist unfolds
from the face of a mountain,
so earth was there.

Such choices, of course, were endless.

One final decision bears highlighting: I have chosen to end this version when the arc of the mythic narrative, as I see it, completes. The dilemma that launches the story onto its course is quite clear: the world must be created and populated with true humans, so that the first day might dawn. Once the sun rises into the sky and this moment has drawn to a close, the mythic arc draws closed as well and a distinct shift occurs. In the remaining pages of the *Popol Vuh*, the focus moves from universal myth to a protohistory and a genealogy of the K'iche' aristocracy, intent on establishing the divine roots of that ruling lineage. While there is much to be discovered in these pages, I fear my imaginary modern reader would find these lists of names and lineages inaccessible and perhaps confounding without footnotes and further context. Thus, as the mythic section of the *Popol Vuh* closes, so does this poem.

A recurring thought spurred me along during this project: the idea that the Americas deserve their own myth, with a living voice in a new idiom. Indeed, they've had their own myth for thousands of years. Often referred to as the "oldest book in America," the *Popol Vuh* is known by many names: the Book of the People, the Book of the Community, the Council Book, the Sacred Book of the Maya. Carlos Fuentes even referred to it as "the Mayan Bible." But the K'iche' etymology of the name offers an image richer than any of these approximations: a metaphor elegant in its simplicity. The words *Popol Vuh* derive, literally, from "the book of the woven mat." The story serves as a meeting place, a mat where people gather to hear its truth be told. The imagery of the book as a piece of weaving evokes both a work of intersecting strands and patterns, and the interwoven fibers of a culture—much as the word "text" derives from the Latin *textus*, meaning a woven thing.

As it has many names, the *Popol Vuh* is also many things: it is a work of startling cosmic perspective, a masterpiece of world literature, a founding myth of the Americas, a heroic epic embedded into the cocoon of a creation story, the proto-history and genealogy of a royal lineage, the seeds of a cosmology, and so on. But first and foremost, the *Popol Vuh* is a rattling good story.

҉

After its brief prologue, the myth opens with a broad sky and a silent sea. All is suspended and in suspense. We then launch into the origins of humanity, beginning with the creation of the earth, a world that springs into being from divine discussion. The gods ponder and wonder and then, much as in the first book of Genesis, creation is literally spoken into existence:

> When it was time to make the earth:
> it only took a word.
> To make earth they said, "Earth."

Yet this green world, for all its lushness, is still incomplete: what has been spoken into existence must return the favor. The gods crave their names to be named—they, too, are fed by words. And so this earth needs peopling. The remainder of the myth's prodigious energy is spent on preparing the world for the birth of humans who can raise their voices to the heavens. For this is the *Popol Vuh*'s test for whether people are truly people: they must speak words that make sense, and thus function as an intelligent mirror of their origin.

Unlike Genesis, however, this world is not the product of a single stentorian voice, but a conversation. This is an act of collaboration. And though the gods engage a number of rough drafts, including people made of mud and figures carved from wood, true humans have yet to be formed and the sun has yet to rise when this creation story is paused, and something like a heroic epic begins.

In this twilight world of pre-sunrise, a pretender has set himself up as a false sun, and order must be restored before creation can proceed. The supernaturally gifted hero twins, Hunahpu and Xbalanque, spring fully formed onto the page to set things right. We do not know from whence they come; they simply walk into the story with their blowguns, ready to confront the folly of false deities. Ultimately, the twins' adventures take them, quite literally, to hell and back, where—like their mythic compatriots Odysseus and Gilgamesh—they touch upon eternity before returning to earth, as the sun and the moon, so that the first day might dawn.

Though the frieze at El Mirador is thousands of years old, part of my fascination with the *Popol Vuh* is how contemporary it can feel to twenty-first-century readers. The narrative loops in and out of time in a way that one is tempted to call postmodern. Though it would seem the creation of the world is a beginning to beget all beginnings, each proceeding episode of the myth spirals further back, to a time before the sun and moon—a time before time—as the myth unhinges from linear progression. The boys walk into the story as youths, their father is born in the ensuing episode, and only then do we learn of their own birth and past adventures. The definition of the divine order is fluid as well, at times seeming to shift from plural to singular, male to female. The creation of the earth is told in present tense, lending vivid immediacy. It is as if we are looking out through the *ilb'al*, and the world is unfurling before our very eyes. But perhaps my favorite moment in the entire epic stems from how it stares mortality in the face—or skull, as it were—something that truly marks the story as eternal.

After outsmarting the lords of the underworld in the climactic triumph that will finally allow true people to be born into the world, Hunahpu and Xbalanque visit the place where the severed head of their father hangs in a calabash tree. It is a compelling image and strange fruit, simultaneously dead and alive. In an attempt to revive him, the twins ask his head to name itself: its mouth, its nose, its eye. This faith in the power of language is touching, as is the image of two boys who, in spite of triumphing over death itself, still look to their father to set things right.

The skull opens its mouth as if to speak, but "little more was said." There is a suspended moment where we sense the boys waiting, just as we waited in the hush before the gods spoke the world into existence. But the skull does not speak of its vacant nose, its hollow stare. It cannot. Mortal vision does not reach beyond the horizon of death. The grasp of our senses will end. It is a breathtaking moment, both cryptic and beautiful, offering a note of quiet emptiness in the midst of exultation. In a world where death is often viewed as an enemy and where the individual voice reigns supreme, clearly the *Popol Vuh* still has much to tell us about ourselves.

Part One

PREAMBLE

The root of the ancient word starts here,
the root of this place called K'iche'.

Here we will write. Here we will plant
the ancient word of the beginning,
the origin of all that was done in the citadel
of K'iche', among the people of K'iche' nation.

Here we will gather what can be shown,
here we will gather what can be made known,
the account of the first sowing and the first dawn
brought by the Framer and the Shaper,
> by the ones who have borne children
> and the ones who have planted them,
> by Hunahpu Possum and Hunahpu Coyote,
> by Great White Peccary and Coatimundi,
> by Sovereign and Quetzal Serpent,
> by Heart of Lake and Heart of Sea,
> by the maker of green earth and the maker of blue sky,
> > as they are called.

All together these are named and known
> as the Grandmother and Grandfather,
> whose names are Xmucane and Xpiyacoc,
> shelterer and defender, twice midwife and twice patriarch,
> > as they are called in K'iche'.

They spoke the world into being
with luminous words and clear truth.

We will write about this now
    amidst talk of God
    under the rule of Christendom.

We will bring it forth
because there is no longer a way
to see the ancient book, the Popol Vuh:

    that way of seeing clearly that came from beside the sea,
    that account of our origins in the shadows,
    that place where we see the dawn of life, as it is said.

The original book exists.
It was written long ago
but those who read and ponder it
have hidden their faces.

∘ ∘ ∘

Now,
the lighting of the sky
and the germination of the earth
takes a while to perform:

its four corners and four sides,
the measuring and staking,
the halving and the stretching
of those cords that contain
the womb of sky and earth.

So the four corners and four sides
were laid out, as it is said,

by the Framer and the Shaper,
mother-father of life and birth,
giver of breath, giver of heart,

those who bear the never-ending light,
those who hearten the sunlit children
    born of woman and man;

they are tender in all things,
the Framer and the Shaper,
they are knowers of all things,
all that there is in sky and earth and lake and sea.

THE BEGINNING

Here we are. All is still.

All is still silent and waiting.
All is silent and calm. Hushed
and empty is the womb of the sky.

These are the first words.
This is the first speaking.

There is not yet one person,
        one animal, bird, fish,
        crab, tree, rock, hollow,
        canyon, field, or woven forest.

The broad sky is all alone.
The face of the earth is not yet here.
The expanse of sea is all alone,
along with the womb of the sky.

Nothing has been gathered.
All is at rest. Nothing stirs.
All is drowsing. Nothing stands.
Only the breadth of water, only the tranquil sea.

There is no thought of what might be.
All lies dark and silent in the only night.

All alone are the Framer and the Shaper,
the Sovereign and the feathered serpent,
        the ones who have borne children
        and the ones who have planted them.

They are luminous in the waters,
wrapped in feathers of quetzal and cotinga.
Brilliance glimmers through the gaps.

And so they are called Quetzal Serpent,
and hold deep wisdom in their bones.

And so they are called Heart of Sky.
And this is said as the name of the god.

o o o

Then came the word.

Heart of Sky arrived
in the dark of the only night.

Heart of Sky arrived
with Sovereign and Quetzal Serpent.

They talked together then.
They pondered and wondered.

They reached an accord,
braiding together their words
        and their thoughts.

They heartened one another
and it came clear: the conception
of humans born beneath a luminous sky.

Then they conceived
the generations of trees
and the generations of thickets,

the germination of all life
in the darkness of pale dawn,
by Heart of Sky, who is called Hurricane.

        Lightning Hurricane is first.
        Newborn Thunderbolt is second.
        Sudden Lightning is third.

These three as one are Heart of Sky.
They came together with Sovereign and Quetzal Serpent.
Their joining conceived both light and life:

"How shall it be sown?
When should dawn come?
Who will feed these worlds?
Who will sustain them?"

"Let it be like this.

Let the water clear away
so the plate of earth
comes toward the light.
Let the land gather
and level out.

Then it can be sown.
Then the dawn can come."

"But there will be no words of praise or prayer
to sing of what we frame and shape
until humanity is born, until true people
have been made," they said.

When it was time to make the earth:
      it only took a word.
      To make earth they said, "Earth"

and there it was: sudden
as a cloud or mist unfolds
from the face of a mountain,
         so earth was there.

Then mountains were called from the water
and instantly the mountains rose.

It was simply their pure spirit,
their glinting spark of insight
that conceived the mountains and the valleys,
whose face grew sudden groves of cypress and pine.

And the feathered serpent was pleased with this:

"It is good you came, Heart of Sky.
Lightning Hurricane, Newborn Thunderbolt,
and you as well, Sudden Lightning.
The shape of our work will turn out well."

And so the earth formed first,
folded in mountains and valleys,
and water channeled the land
and streams threaded the slopes,
divided by the land as it rose.

This was the formation of things
called forth by Heart of Sky and Heart of Earth,
as they are called, for they were the first to conceive it.

The sky was set apart
and the earth was set apart within the water.
So the world was made complete
when they pondered and they wondered.

THE CREATION OF ANIMALS

Now they conceived
the animals of the mountains,
the guardians of the forests,
and all that lived there:
  the deer and the birds,
  the puma and the jaguar,
  the serpent and the rattler,
  the pit viper and the keepers of the wood.

Then the ones who have borne children
and the ones who have planted them asked:

"Why should rustling silence
live alone beneath the trees?"

"Better that there be guardians," they said,

and sudden as they spoke these thoughts
  the deer and birds were there.

When this was done, they gave them homes:

"You, the deer, will sleep beside coursing rivers
deep in canyons. Your herds will increase
among the meadows and the branching forest
where you will stand and walk on your own four limbs."

Then they established nests for birds, both large and small:

"You, the birds, will make your homes
high in the treetops and nestled in the bush.
Your flocks will increase, like leaves among branches."

Once this was done, all received their place of rest.

And so homes were given
to the animals of earth and sky

by She who has borne children
and He who has planted them.

Thus all was made complete for the deer and the birds.

∘ ∘ ∘

Then the Framer and the Shaper
and She who has borne children
and He who has planted them
        said to the deer and birds:

"Talk. Speak. No moaning, no cries.
        It's time to speak to one another now,
        each among its own kind, its own group,"
        so they told the deer and the birds,
        the pumas and jaguars and serpents.

"Name our names, praise us.
We are your mother, we are your father.

        Say it this way:

'Hurricane,
Newborn Thunderbolt and Sudden Lightning,
Heart of Sky and Heart of Earth,
Framer and Shaper,
She who has borne children
and He who has planted them.'

Call our names. Keep our days.
Speak our prayers. Sing to us."

But it did not happen
that they spoke like people.

They merely squawked and chittered.
They merely howled and roared.

Language did not show its face.
Each cried out its different sound.

The Framer and the Shaper heard this,
and they spoke among themselves,

"This has not turned out well.
They have not named our names.
We are their Framer and their Shaper.
                    This will not do."

So they told them:

"This must be changed. It has not happened
that you spoke like people, and so we change our word.

What you eat and what sustains you,
where you sleep and the lands around you—
whatever is yours will remain in the canyons and forests.

Though you were unable to name our names
or speak our praise and honor our days,

there may yet be someone else to call upon us,
a giver of praise whom we have not yet made.
So this must be your service: let your flesh be eaten."

      They told this to the animals,
      large and small, on the face of the earth.

   o o o

And so once again
      they wanted to test chance,
      they wanted to risk another attempt,
      they wanted to try their thoughts
           at making one to honor them.

The animals did not make speech
and so the work was not complete
and so their flesh was then brought low.
The animals were made to serve,
killed and eaten on the face of the earth.

FIGURES OF MUD AND FIGURES OF WOOD

And so it was time
for another attempt
at the human design

by the Framer and the Shaper,
by She who has borne children
and He who has planted them:

"Let us simply try again
            for soon it shall be sown,
            soon the dawn will come.

Let us make one who provides,
let us make one who sustains us.

How else will we be called upon?
How else will we be remembered
                on the face of the earth?

We have already made a first attempt
at this framing and this shaping,

but no one named our names,
no one spoke our praise or kept our days.

So let us try again
to make one who gives praise,
to make one who provides and sustains."

So then came the forming
of earth and mud into flesh.

But they saw it was not good.
The work separated and crumbled.
The work softened into mush.
The body loosened and dissolved.

The head rose thick
from the shoulders.

The face was mashed.
The gaze was fixed.

It could not turn
and look about.

And then it spoke
and made no sense.

It melted quickly,
dipped in water.

Then the Framer and the Shaper said:
"This mistake will fall away.
It cannot walk. It bears no seed.

Let it dwindle and be forgotten.
Let it dwindle to an afterthought."

So then they let it come undone.

They toppled what they'd framed and shaped.

And they said:

"How then will we truly frame
one that will grow to name our names
and walk the earth and honor us?"

And then they considered.

"Let us simply call upon
        Xpiyacoc and Xmucane,
        Hunahpu Possum and Hunahpu Coyote
        to read the days, divine the time,"
                        they said to themselves.

        And so they called,
                "Grandmother of Day,
                Grandmother of Light!"

                For this is how they called the seers,
                Xpiyacoc and Xmucane,
                to gaze into the days beyond.

o o o

Hurricane then spoke
with Sovereign and Quetzal Serpent

and they called upon
the ones who keep the days, the ones who see beyond,

"Let it be uncovered. Let it be found
        how we will frame true people,
        how we will shape the ones
        who will sustain and nurture us.

Let our names be named and remembered,
        for it is through words that we are fed.

                Midwife, Patriarch,
                Grandmother, Grandfather,
                Xmucane, Xpiyacoc—

so let it be called! Let it be sown. Let it dawn

                that we are known,
                that we are sustained,
                that we are invoked

by model people, by human figures, the human form.

Reveal your names: Hunahpu Possum and Hunahpu Coyote,
                She who has borne children and He who
                        has planted them,
                Great Peccary and Great Coati,
                Precious Stone Worker and Jeweler,
                Woodcarver and Carpenter,
                Maker of Green Earth and Shaper of
                        Blue Sky,
                Incense Maker and Master of Craft,
                Grandmother of Day and Grandmother
                        of Light.

These names are called
for our human work, for what we frame and shape.

Cast out your grains of yellow maize,
Cast out your true-red tz'ite seeds.

Let them tumble in the light,
let them tell how things will turn
when we gouge and carve a face in wood,"
             so they said, to those who keep the days.

And so began the casting and the telling,
             the counting and revealing,
             the hand moving over the grains,
             the seeds, the lots, the days.

Then they spoke, the one Grandmother, the one Grandfather—

       for this is Grandfather, the tz'ite master, called Xpiyacoc,

       and this is Grandmother,
             who sits at the foot and shapes the days,
       called Xmucane—

       they said, as they cast the days:

"Let it be uncovered.
       Let it be found. Say it.
       Our open ears wait listening.

       Let the tree be found

that will be crafted and carved
by the Framer and Shaper.

If this will be the one
who nurtures and sustains,
then let it be sown.
Then let the dawn come.

You grains of maize,
you tz'ite seeds,
you hold the days,

so you are called.
We summon you."

So it was spoken to the yellow maize.
So it was spoken to the true-red seeds.

"Finish it off, Heart of Sky.
No more hard lessons
for Sovereign and Quetzal Serpent.
Don't grind their faces in it."

Then they spoke it straight:

"Let these figures carved from wood
come out well. Let these wooden figures
talk and speak on the face of the earth."

"So be it," they said.

And sudden as they spoke these thoughts
the figures carved from wood were
there: human in form, speaking human tongues.

They made daughters and sons
and peopled the whole face of the earth.

But their hearts were blank, their minds hollow.
They held no memory of who had made them.
They crawled and ambled aimlessly.
They could not remember Heart of Sky.

And so another attempt fell away,
a mere stab at making humankind:

They talked at first, with shriveled faces.
Their legs and arms were withered sticks.

No river of blood flowed through
their limbs. They had no sweat, no oil.

Their cheeks were dry, their faces masks.
Their bodies stiff, they did not yield,

and so they showed no understanding
before the Framer and the Shaper
who gave them birth and gave them heart.

They were the first people
to crowd the face of the earth.

THE FLOOD

So they were crushed,
the figures of wood.

They were splintered
and demolished.

Heart of Sky devised a flood
to thunder down upon their heads.

Man had been carved of tz'ite wood,
  by the Framer and the Shaper,
and Woman woven of reeds,

but their eyes held no light
and their tongues did not speak
before the ones who made them
and so they were finished by the flood:

Rain came down, thick as resin,

bringing face-gougers
who gashed out their eyes,

bringing death-blades
who severed their skulls,

bringing Crunching Jaguar
who tore at their flesh,

bringing Striking Jaguar
who slit them clean open.

They smashed bones,
they shredded tendons.

They pulverized them into bits.
They ground their faces into strips

because there was no gleam
of understanding in their eyes

before their mother and their father,
Heart of Sky, named Hurricane.

So the face of the earth went black:

a black rain fell all day, all night,
and animals both large and small
began to slink into their homes—

their faces were crushed
by trees and stones—

and everything began to speak,
tortilla slabs and water jars,
their plates and cooking pots,
their dogs and grinding stones—
            everything tore into them.

Their dogs and turkeys said:

"Pain was all
  you offered us.
  You ate our flesh.
  Now it's our turn."

Then the grinding stones said:

"You wore us down.
    Every day at dusk and dawn
    with a r-r-rasping shred
    and a shr-shr-shredding rasp
    you ground our faces in it.

    This is what we gave
    when you were first people,
    but today you'll feel our power.

    We'll grind your flesh into a paste.
    We'll pound you down like meal."

Then the dogs said this to them:

"Why did you never
    feed us our food?
    All we did was look at you

    and you flung us out,
    you chased us away.
    You held a stick

    whenever you ate,

to bring it thudding
down upon us.

That was how
you spoke with us.

We could not talk
and so got nothing.

How could you not know
we skulked behind you,

wasting away?
In truth you did know—

so on this day, now,
you have the chance

to try our teeth,
in our mouths.

We will eat you."

And so they tore into them and ravaged their faces.

Then the cooking slabs and the pots spoke:

"Pain was all
you gave to us:

Soot in our mouths,
soot in our faces.

You threw us into
blistering fire.

We are insensible
to scorching pain,

so why not try it
for yourselves?

We will burn you."

And so they had their faces crushed—

the hearthstones
and the cooking slabs
leapt from the fire,

they shot from flames
and flattened them—
smashing their skulls:

pain was all they gave.

So the first people fled.
They ran like hell.

They tried climbing onto their houses
but their houses collapsed and bucked them off.

They tried climbing into the treetops
but the heaving limbs just sagged and bent.

They tried to enter into caves
but the hillsides closed their mouths.

So the first people were undone.
They were demolished, overthrown.

They were ruined and crushed:
their mouths, their faces, all of them.

o o o

It is said that their descendants
now live in the forest as monkeys,

because their flesh was merely wood
when they were framed and shaped.

And so the monkeys look like us,
a remnant of that earlier work,
a wooden echo of our kind.

Part Two

SEVEN MACAW

All this was back when light
barely dimmed the air with early dawn.

There was no sun. But there was one
who puffed himself up named Seven Macaw.

Sky and earth were there
but the sun and moon
merely flickered in clouds.

So Seven Macaw set himself up
as a bright sign for those first people,
before the flood drowned them.

In his essence, he was like
one who has been enchanted:

"I dwell supreme
        above the heads
        of these people
        framed and shaped.

    I am the sun
    to light their days.
    I am the moon
    to mark their months.

    Great is my light:

by the precious glow
of my silver and gold
I illuminate the way.

My gaze sparkles
with glimmering turquoise.
My teeth flash grins
that shimmer with jade.

My face shines brilliant as the sky
and holds my beak
gleaming like a distant moon.

My throne is silver and gold.
I brighten the face of the earth
whenever I step forth.

So I am the sun,
as well as the moon,
for all children born
beneath my light.

So be it.
My vision is vast,"
                            said Seven Macaw.

Now, Seven Macaw
was not truly the sun.

He only puffed his plumage
and polished his precious metals.

His gaze did not reach
much beyond his own perch.

His vision did not touch
everything beneath the face of the sky.

This was before the glow of the sun
could truly be seen, before the moon and stars.

So Seven Macaw slung his boasts
about lighting the months and days
before the dawn had even come.

He hungered only for greatness.
He wanted total dominion
before the light of the sun came clear.

∘ ∘ ∘

Now we will tell how Seven Macaw died,

how he was defeated in those days
back when the figures of wood
were shattered in the flood.

THE FALL OF SEVEN MACAW

This is the root of his defeat,
This is how his day was shaken
by the twins, named Hunahpu and Xbalanque.

The boys were gods and saw
how his pride swelled into evil,
fed by desire beneath Heart of Sky.

So the boys said:

"No good will come of this.

True people will never live
on the face of such an earth.

So let's take aim
with our blowguns.

Let's shoot him while he glides
above the limbs, hungry for food.

Let's send a sickness into him
so all his jade and precious metals,
all his jewels and glittering baubles,

and all he lifts his eyes to see
will come to nothing.

True people cannot be born
in a world where flaming splendor
lies only in silver and gold.

So let it be done."

They shouldered their blowguns
as they said these words.

  ° ° °

Now, this Seven Macaw had two sons:

The firstborn was Zipacna,
the second Cabracan—

Chimalmat was their mother,
the wife of Seven Macaw.

Zipacna was a mountain-builder,
a sustainer of great volcanoes:

Chigag,
Hunahpu,
Peculya,
Xcanul,
Macambo,
Huliznab,

these are the names of mountains,
the open mouths of fire
that existed when it first dawned.

Zipacna made them all in a single night.

Cabracan was a mountain-shaker,
big or small, he made them tremble.

They too were swollen with pride,
the sons of Seven Macaw.

"Here I am.
 I am the sun!"
            said Seven Macaw.

"Here I am.
 I made the earth!"
            said Zipacna.

"And look at me!
 I knock down sky
 and make mountains crumble,"
            said Cabracan.

They were truly the sons of Seven Macaw.
Their greatness was the same sort as his.

Hunahpu and Xbalanque saw this clearly,
            how such grasping evil

kept our first mother and our first father
from being brought to life.

So they laid plans and plotted
death and disappearance.

THE SHOOTING OF SEVEN MACAW

So here is Seven Macaw,
and here is the great nance tree.

He soars every day among its limbs
to seek its yellow fruit.

Hunahpu and Xbalanque
have seen this,

and so they keep their quiet vigil
beneath the tree.

They are hidden there
now, among the lace of leaves.

When Seven Macaw arrives,
gliding to his perch above his meal,
this is where he is shot:

Hunahpu aimed his blowgun
straight at Seven Macaw's
jaw and it broke open

in a piercing cry. He plunged
over the treetops, thumped
beak-down on the ground.

Hunahpu sprinted, eager
to seize him, but it was his arm
that was seized and torn
clean off by Seven Macaw.

He wrenched it straight back,
bent it at the shoulder until
it ripped free from Hunahpu.

> Still, it was good what they did.
> The first round was not the full battle,

> though it is true Hunahpu's arm
> was taken home by Seven Macaw.

He arrived there with his jaw
cradled gently in his palms.

"What have you got there?"
asked his wife, Chimalmat.
> "What is it?"

"Two maniacs shot me
and dislocated my jaw!
They cracked and loosened my teeth!
The pain is a torment!

So let me just hang
what I've brought here
over the fire. Let it dangle

there, above the flames,
until those conniving demons
try to come and get it."

      As Seven Macaw said this
      he hung Hunahpu's arm on a hook.

o o o

In the meantime,
Hunahpu and Xbalanque
were making plans.

They went to speak
with the first Grandfather,
whose hair was truly white,

and with the first Grandmother,
whose eyes were truly humble.

They walked bent over now.
They were already ancient.

Great White Peccary
  was the name of the Grandfather.
Great White Coati
  was the name of the Grandmother.

The boys then said to them:

"Please come with us now
when we go to fetch our arm from Seven Macaw.
We'll just follow along behind you.
You can say to him:

> 'Please put up with our grandsons
>   that follow along behind us.
> Their mother and father are dead,
>   so they have to tag along.
> We provide for them by pulling
>   worms from people's teeth.'

Then he will simply see us as children
even though we'll be feeding you ideas."

"Very well," answered the Grandparents
        and then off they went.

o o o

Seven Macaw was perched
on the edge of his throne.

Grandmother and Grandfather
wandered the woods beneath his home,
the boys scampering behind them.

Seven Macaw's jaw kept breaking
into groans because of his teeth.

When he saw them traveling along,
he hollered, "Where are you
coming from, my grandparents?"

"We're just making a living, my lord."

"How do you provide for yourselves?
Aren't those your children behind you?"

"No, they are not, my lord.
These are our grandsons.
We must live to take pity on them.
They always receive a portion,
my lord, what scraps we can give."

The lord was nearly shattered
by tooth-pain now: it took some work
to speak these next words:

"I beg you, please, take pity on me.
What potions would you make?
What medicines might cure me?"

"We simply remove worms from teeth,
and cure bad eyes, and set bones, my lord,"
replied the Grandmother and Grandfather.

"Very well. Then cure my teeth.
They ache all day. I can't stand it.
I can't sleep. My eyes ache too.

Two maniacs shot me with a blowgun.
I haven't been able to eat since.

So take pity on my jaw and my teeth:
my mouth is the source of all my agony."

"Very well, my lord.
It's gnawing worms that cause this pain.
We'll simply have to replace them.
Your teeth will have to come out."

"But maybe that's not so good.
It is my glittering teeth and eyes
that make me the lord that I am.
They are my finery—"

"We must be certain to replace them, then.
Here, we have some fine ground bone."

But instead of bone, it was simply white
grains of maize they held in their hands.

"Very good. Take them out, then. Help me!"

So the teeth of Seven Macaw were yanked
and replaced by white grains of maize:
his mouth nothing but a grin of corn.

His face fell in an instant.
No one took him for a lord.

They wrenched the brilliant jade
and gleaming turquoise from his mouth.

They worked a cure on his eyes
as well. They plucked them out.
They scoured his face of shining gold.

Still, he didn't feel much pain.
He was left with a hollow stare
as his greatness was stripped clean.

This was their plan, Hunahpu and Xbalanque.

Before long Seven Macaw died,
and Hunahpu went to get his arm.
Chimalmat was dead as well,
the wife of Seven Macaw.

So the wealth of Seven Macaw
was taken away by simple healers:

the jewels and precious stones,
all that had swelled him with pride
here on the face of the earth.

The enchanted Grandmother
and the enchanted Grandfather
were the ones who did it.

Then the boys took the arm
and planted it back in its socket
where it grew good once again.

They had desired the end of Seven Macaw
and so they made it come about,
bringing low his loathsome pride.

Then they ran off again, two boys
who'd done the word of Heart of Sky.

ZIPACNA AND THE FOUR HUNDRED BOYS

Here, now, are the deeds of Zipacna,
the firstborn son of Seven Macaw,
who said, "I am the maker of mountains."

Zipacna was bathing in the river
when four hundred boys passed by
dragging a tree, a beam for their hut.

The four hundred boys walked along
with the huge trunk they had cut
for the lintel of their dwelling.

Zipacna came up to them
and asked, "What are you doing?"

"It's just this tree.
We cannot heft it
onto our shoulders."

"I will carry it on my shoulders.
Where does it go? What use
do your hearts intend for it?"

"Merely the lintel of our hut."

"Very good," he said,

and he hoisted it onto his shoulders
and carried it up to the opening
of the hut of the four hundred boys.

"Why not stay with us, boy?
 Do you have a mother and father?"

"There is no one," he said.

"Then we could surely use your help.
 Tomorrow we will raise another
 trunk as a beam for our hut."

"Very good," he said again.

Then the four hundred boys gathered
their thoughts and spoke together:

"This boy, what will we do with him?"

"We should kill him.
It's not good what he does,
how he lifts up those huge logs all by himself."

"Let's dig a great hole
and abandon him in the pit."

"We can say to him:
'Go dig out the earth
from the bottom of the hole'

and when he's down there,
hunched in the pit, we can
hurl a great tree trunk . . ."

". . . and he will die down there,"
said the four hundred boys.

So they dug a huge pit
that went down deep,
and they called Zipacna.

"We're calling on you
to go digging down there
because we cannot do it."

"Sounds good," he said,
and crawled into the hole.

"Shout once you've dug it out
and gotten yourself in deep."

"Fine," he said.
Then he started digging.

But the hole he dug
was for his own salvation.

He suddenly sensed
he was to be killed,

and dug a branching hole
that tunneled to one side,
a second hole that saved him.

"How far have you gotten into it?"
asked the four hundred boys.

"I'm digging quickly.
When I call up to you,
you'll know the hole is dug," hollered Zipacna.

He did not dig
a grave for his burial,
but a place to put his life.

So when he called up to them
he was already safe inside his hole.

"Come and take the dirt,
the loose earth I dug out.
I've gone down truly deep.

Perhaps you cannot hear my call?

Your voices are only
echoes in the distance.
They have a hollow ring,"

said Zipacna, from the depths
where he now took shelter.

Meanwhile, the boys had dragged
a massive log to the edge of the pit.

They hurled it down into the hole.

"Is he no more?
He does not speak."

"Once we hear him crack
open in a piercing cry,
we will know he is dead,"
they said to each other.

They spoke in whispers,
from the places where they
had hidden their faces.

Then he let loose a wail,
Zipacna cried out one last word
when the tree struck bottom.

"Yes! Success!"

"We got him. He's dead."

"This is truly good."

"What kind of omen would it be
if he had kept doing those deeds?
If he had persisted in his work?"

"He would have become first among us."

"He would have placed himself over us—
Even us, the four hundred boys!"

And so they rejoiced.

"Time to make sweet drink!
For three days, that's all we'll make."

"Once three days pass,
 we will drink to our dwelling—"

        "Our hut!"

"We'll toast ourselves,
the four hundred boys!" they said.

"And tomorrow we'll see,
and the next day we'll see
if lines of ants don't come
simmering from the earth
when he starts to stink and rot.

Then our hearts will rest in comfort
while we drain our sweet drink," they said.

Zipacna heard all this from his hole.

And the second day came
and the ants convened,
crawling and swarming.

They trailed under the log,
gathering the hair of Zipacna
as well as the nails of Zipacna
to carry everywhere in their teeth.

When the boys saw this,
they said to one another:

"He's finished, that demon!"

"Look at the ants swarm the hole.
They assembled in a crawling horde
and now they're trailing everywhere
carrying bits of hair in their teeth."

"And those must be his fingernails!"

        "We did it, at last!"

But Zipacna was still alive.

He had simply plucked his hair
and gnawed away his nails
and given them to the ants.

Yet the four hundred boys
were certain he was dead.

So when the third day came,
they laid into the sweet drink.

They got drunk, those boys,
all four hundred of them.
They couldn't feel a thing.

That was when Zipacna
collapsed their hut
and crushed their heads.

They were finished,
struck down, all of them.
Not even one or two
were saved among four hundred.

And so the four hundred boys
were killed by Zipacna,
the son of Seven Macaw.

o o o

It is said these boys became
a clustered constellation
some call the Little Crowd

but perhaps these words
are merely toying with us.

Now, we will tell how Zipacna died
how he was overthrown by the twins,
          Hunahpu and Xbalanque.

THE DEFEAT OF ZIPACNA

So this is the death of Zipacna,
his defeat at the hands of the twins,
Hunahpu and Xbalanque.

Their hearts were offended
by how Zipacna brought about
the death of the four hundred boys.

    o o o

Fish and crabs were all he ate.
He searched for them in rivers.

All day long he wandered streams
seeking out his only food.

All night long he walked the dark
carrying mountains on his back.

So Hunahpu and Xbalanque
fashioned an enormous crab for him.

They picked bromeliads
that blossom in the forest,
huge blooms strung thick on vines.

These became the arms they used,
the buds split open into claws.

A hollowed stone became its shell.
It clacked against the ground.

They put the crab into a cave
under a mountain, called Meauan.

Then the boys came along
and found Zipacna at the river.

"Where are you going, boy?"
        they asked Zipacna.

"I'm not going anywhere.
I'm just looking for food."

"What's your food?"
"Just fish and crabs.
But I can't find any right now.

It's been two days since I last fed
and now my hunger is eating me,"
        said Zipacna to the twins.

"There is a crab, down below the canyon—
        a truly enormous one!
Why don't you try your chances with it?

Maybe you'd be able to eat it!

It kept biting at us
when we tried to grab it
and we were afraid. If it's still there—

you could catch it!"

"Take pity on me, boys.
Come and show me the way!" said Zipacna.

"We don't want to—
you go on yourself.

There is no way to get lost
if you simply follow the river.

When you are standing below
a great mountain, there you are:
it will be at the foot of the canyon,"
                                    said Hunahpu and Xbalanque.

"Please, boys, take pity!
What if it can't be found?
You lead the way and I'll follow.

There are surely birds along the way.
You could shoot them with your blowguns.
I know their hiding places . . ."

He humbled himself, promising rewards,
and began to cry before the boys.

"You might not be able to catch it,"
                                    said the boys.

"You might have to turn back, like we did.
Not only could we not eat it—it bit us.

We crawled in headfirst, on our bellies,
but it quickly climbed away in fear.

A little later, we inched in on our backs,
so we could reach up to grab it,
but we could not find it again.

So it's better to slide in on your back."

"Fine," said Zipacna.

So they went, accompanied by Zipacna,
and arrived at the cave below the canyon

where their ruse lay waiting,
the crab, gleaming bright red.

"Looks good," rejoiced Zipacna.

He was nearly finished with hunger,
he wanted to plunge in and eat it,
already tasting the meat in his mouth.

He bolted in headfirst, on his belly,
but the crab scuttled high into the cave,
        so Zipacna pulled out.

"You didn't get it?" asked the boys.

"No. It clambered up into the rocks.
After a while I couldn't find it again.
Perhaps I should slide in on my back."

So he entered the cave again.
He inched all the way in until
only his kneecaps were showing.
He was completely swallowed up.

Then the great mountain settled
down upon his chest, pinning him

so that Zipacna couldn't turn
into anything but stone.

o o o

This was the defeat of Zipacna,
at the hands of Hunahpu and Xbalanque,
the so-called "Maker of Mountains,"
the first son of Seven Macaw.

He was defeated beneath a mountain,
Meauan is its name.

It was simply enchantment
that overthrew this second one
puffed full of his own pride.

Now, we will tell the tale of another.

THE DEFEAT OF CABRACAN

The third one swollen with pride
was the second son of Seven Macaw,

Cabracan was his name.
"I am the wrecker of mountains," he said.

Only Hunahpu and Xbalanque
could have overthrown this Cabracan.

So Hurricane, Newborn Thunderbolt,
and Sudden Lightning came to them, and said:

"According to my word
another must be defeated:
the second son of Seven Macaw.

It is not good what they have done
here on the face of the earth.

They exceed the sun
in the heft of their greatness,
and this is not how things should be.

So lure him away—there!
to the place where the sun rises,"
said Hurricane, to the twins.

"Very good, my lord.
The truth has always been
that we see no good in him.

He does not belong with you,
raised up with Heart of Sky,"
            the twins replied
                to the word of Hurricane.

                ° ° °

In the meantime, Cabracan
persisted in wrecking mountains.

With merely the slightest tap of his foot
the face of the earth would crumble down.
Great mountains, small mountains, no matter.
Then the twins came to meet him.

"Where are you going, boy?"
                they asked Cabracan.

"I'm not going anywhere.
I just demolish mountains.
I'll smash them as long as the sun shines,"
                said Cabracan.

"So, where did you two come from?
I do not know your faces.
Tell me, what are your names?" he asked.

"We have no names. We simply
hunt and trap in the mountains.

We're just poor orphans,
with nothing that is ours, boy.
We wander the mountains, great and small.

There was one mountain we saw
growing beyond all others.

It just keeps rising into the sky,
beyond the clouds, surpassing every peak.

There wasn't even a single bird
to hunt upon its face. Is it true

that you can fell any mountain, boy?"
asked Hunahpu and Xbalanque.

"It can't be true you saw this mountain.
Where is it? You will see beyond a doubt
I'll knock it down. Where did you see it?"

"Over there, in the place where the sun rises,"
said Hunahpu and Xbalanque.

"Good. Lead the way, and I'll follow!"

"Why not just walk between us—
one on your right hand, the other your left?—
because we're stalking with our blowguns.

If there are birds, we'll shoot them," they said.

Shooting their blowguns
gave them great joy.

The twins practiced shooting
without any clay pellets.

They shot down many birds
blowing only bolts of air.
Cabracan watched, amazed.

The boys then spun out a fire
using a twisting drill of wood,
to roast the birds above the flames.

They coated one with quick-lime,
cloaking its skin with white earth.

"This is the one we will give to him
when he's ravenous with hunger.

When he savors the aroma,
then we'll know he is undone.

The earth will bake into its skin,
and we will cook it in the earth.

Thus he will be buried, just so,
in the same way beneath the dirt.

This is how the great sage
will come to be framed and shaped.

Then it can be sown.
Then the dawn can come," said the twins.

"Cabracan will be inflamed
to feed upon the flesh we cook.
He'll hunger with his very heart!"
            said Hunahpu and Xbalanque.

Then they roasted the birds,
cooking them a golden brown,
until fat crackled and dripped from their skins,
wafting a fragrant aroma.

Now Cabracan wanted to be fed.
He gulped as the juices rose
and his mouth began to water.

He drooled threads of saliva
because of those fragrant birds,
and then started in begging:

"What is that you're eating?
That aroma is truly delicious.
Give me a little, then . . . ," he said.

So they gave the bird to Cabracan,
and he devoured his own defeat.

Once he'd finished the bird,
they once again went on their way

until they arrived in the east
where the great mountain rose.

But the arms and legs of Cabracan
were weakened now, his muscles
were worn and threadbare.

His strength had left him
for good, because of the earth
on the skin of that bird.

So he couldn't do anything
to the mountains,

he didn't succeed
in smashing them apart.

The twins tied him up then,
knotting his wrists behind his back
and binding his ankles tight.

They hurled him down into the earth
and buried him beneath its weight.

Sometimes, we still feel him twitch.

o o o

So Cabracan was overthrown
by Hunahpu and Xbalanque.

Their deeds cannot be counted
here on the face of the earth.

Now, we will trace the thread back.
Now, we will tell of their birth,

since we've already told
how Seven Macaw was defeated,
along with Zipacna and Cabracan,
here on the face of the earth.

Part Three

THE STORY OF THE FATHER OF HUNAHPU
AND XBALANQUE

Now, we will name the name
of the father of Hunahpu and Xbalanque.
We will retell the tale, from the source.

We will simply repeat
the telling of how it was,
how Hunahpu and Xbalanque came to be.

But we'll only tell it in part,
just a piece,
the story of their father.

∘ ∘ ∘

This, then, is the account
of One Hunahpu and Seven Hunahpu,
for so they are called.

In the darkness of night
One Hunahpu and Seven Hunahpu

were born to their parents,
Xpiyacoc and Xmucane.

Now, this One Hunahpu
had two children, two sons,

the firstborn was called One Batz,
whose name means clever monkey.

The second was called One Chouen,
whose name means nimble maker.

Their mother was named Xbaquiyalo,
so she was called, One Hunahpu's wife.

Seven Hunahpu had no wife.

A helpful boy in his nature,
he lived simply as a companion,
a second self to One Hunahpu.

They knew the world well
and great was their knowledge.

They were visionary seers
on the face of the earth,
and their natures held
the goodness of their birth.

They revealed their true
spark of inventiveness

to the sons of One Hunahpu,
to One Batz and One Chouen,

who became flautists and singers,
and writers and stone-carvers,
and artisans of jade and precious metal.

As for One Hunahpu and Seven Hunahpu,
they spent the length of their days
throwing dice and playing ball.

They would oppose one another
in pairs, four in all, there on the ballcourt.

A falcon often came to watch,
a messenger from Hurricane.

The face of the earth was not far for him,
neither was Xibalba, the underworld.

His sudden flight could take him
up in an instant to Heart of Sky.

○ ○ ○

After the death of Xbaquiyalo,
the mother of One Batz and One Chouen,

the four of them lingered behind
here on the face of the earth,

playing ball on the path
that led down to Xibalba.

So it was that the lords of Xibalba
One Death and Seven Death
heard the ruckus and said:

"What's happening up there
on the surface of the earth?
All that stomping and shouting?

It is time to summon them
to come play ball down here,
so that we might defeat them.

They have no proper sense of place.
They've clearly failed to honor us.
They have no respect, no shame.

The arrogance of such actions
on the roof over our heads!"
said the lords of Xibalba.

So they gathered their thoughts,
One Death and Seven Death,

and they gathered their lords,
great judges all of them,

each unflinching in his task,
each given his own dominion
by One Death and Seven Death.

First, there were the lords
Flying Scab and Gathered Blood
tasked with sickening the veins.

Then come the lords
Pus Demon and Jaundice Fiend
tasked with swelling limbs until

pus seeps from cracked skin
and yellow sickness drains the face,
jaundice, as it is called.

This, then, is the dominion
of Pus Demon and Jaundice Fiend.

Then come the lords
Bone Lance and Skull Staff
who bear the scepters of Xibalba.

Their staves are merely bone.

These are the staff bearers
who skeletalize a body:
they strip away the shreds of flesh

until someone is bone and skull
and dies an emaciated rack
with a bloated belly.

This, then, is the dominion
of Bone Lance and Skull Staff.

Then come the lords
Filth Demon and Puncture Fiend
tasked with overwhelming those

who abandon their rubbish
and the dregs of swept garbage
behind their yards and houses.

Those who do this are caught
and stabbed until they fall
face-to-face with a filthy death.

This, then, is the dominion
of Filth Demon and Puncture Fiend.

Then come the lords
Wingspan and Packstrap.

Their dominion is the sudden death
of those who die on the road,

their mouths frothing red
as they fall, vomiting blood.

Each person must heft a task,
a burden carried on the shoulders;

these lords wear down the neck
and burst the heart within the chest

so a person tumbles in the road,
walking outside in the sunlight,
as suddenly these lords arrive.

This, then, is the dominion
of Wingspan and Packstrap.

These are the ones that gathered
with thoughts of persecution and harassment
for One Hunahpu and Seven Hunahpu.

These lords of Xibalba eyed the gaming things
of One Hunahpu and Seven Hunahpu:

they desired their leathers and arm-bracers,
their yoked-belts and headdresses,
their face-masks and their finery.

◦ ◦ ◦

So now we will tell of the journey
down to the halls of Xibalba.

One Batz and One Chouen
will remain behind.

Their mother has died
and they are now destined

to fall at the hands
of Hunahpu and Xbalanque.

THE SUMMONS TO XIBALBA

In flew the messengers
of One Death and Seven Death:

"Go now, you warrior-lords,
go summon One Hunahpu and Seven Hunahpu,
say to them when you arrive:

'The lords have proclaimed:
        You must come!

        We wish you to come
        play ball with us here

        so we might be enlivened
        and revive the color in our cheeks.

        We are truly amazed by you,
        so you must come!'

Have them bring their implements,
their yoked-belts and arm-bracers,
and the steady beat of their rubber ball.

So we have spoken.
Tell them this when you arrive,"
        the lords said to the messengers.

Their messengers were owls—
　　　Arrow Owl, One-Legged Owl,
　　　Macaw Owl, Skull Owl—
so the messengers of Xibalba are called.

Arrow Owl
pierces like a blade.

One-Legged Owl
bears one wicked talon
beneath two silent wings.

Macaw Owl
has a blood-red back
between his dark wingspan.

Skull Owl
is simply a naked skull

without any legs,
gliding on two dark wings.

These were the four warrior-lords,
messengers bearing a burden.
They came soaring from Xibalba

arriving suddenly over the ballcourt,
where One Hunahpu and Seven Hunahpu

played ball. Honor and Respect
is the name of the place, at Carchah.

The owls perched there
on the stone wall above the court,

where they framed, in order, the words of

     One Death,
     Seven Death,

     Pus Demon,
     Jaundice Fiend,

     Bone Lance,
     Skull Staff,

     Flying Scab,
     Gathered Blood,

     Filth Demon,
     Puncture Fiend,

     Wingspan,
     Packstrap.

These are the names of all the lords
and the owls repeated every word.

"Do you mark these words
from One Death and Seven Death?

Every word is what they spoke.
So we will guide you, as companions.
'Bring all the gaming things,' they said."

"Very well, but wait a moment
while we leave behind a few
instructions for our mother,"
said One Hunahpu and Seven Hunahpu.

So they went home to speak
with their mother, alone,
since their father had died.

"We have to go, mother.
The messengers of the lords
have just arrived to take us.

'You must come,' we were told.
This was the summons
spoken by the messengers.

But we'll leave our rubber ball behind."

Then they climbed and tied it
snug under the roof of their hut.

"You'll hear its steady beat again—
we will play once we've returned."

Then they told One Batz and One Chouen:
"You two be sure to play the flute,
and sing your songs, and write and carve.

You'll be the ones to warm the home,
as well as the heart of your grandmother."

So the boys were instructed,
but Xmucane wept bitterly.

"It is certain we must go, but
we won't die. Do not grieve,"
said One Hunahpu and Seven Hunahpu, as they left.

THE DESCENT INTO XIBALBA

One Hunahpu and Seven Hunahpu
took to the road, guided by the messengers.

They descended the path to Xibalba,
down the steep steps at its mouth
until they emerged in the canyons beyond.

They passed along turbulent rivers
through canyons that trembled and muttered,
named Shivering Canyon and Murmuring Canyon.

They forded the turbulent rivers
and crossed the Scorpion Rapids,
where countless scorpions churned—yet they were not stung.

They arrived at a river of dark blood,
and passed through without drinking.

They arrived at a river thick with pus,
and passed through again, undaunted.

Then they arrived where four roads crossed,
and this Crossroads was their undoing.

One road was red, another was black.
One road was white, the other was yellow.

They stared at the four roads, then
black road spoke and said: "Take me."

"I am the road of the lord," said the road.

This was where they were defeated,
starting down that road to Xibalba.

When they arrived at the council
of the lords of Xibalba,
again they were undone.

The lords who had been seated first
were simply figures carved from wood,
embellished by the Xibalbans.

These, then, were the ones they greeted:

"How do you do, One Death,"
they greeted the dummy.

"Good morning, Seven Death,"
they said to the carved wood.

So they did not prevail
and the Xibalban lords began to roar.

They rumbled with laughter, all of them,
because they had already won the day.

In their hearts, they had defeated
One Hunahpu and Seven Hunahpu.

They kept laughing until finally
One Death and Seven Death said:

"It's so good you've come.
Tomorrow you'll strap on your
yoked-belts and your arm-bracers.

In the meantime," they told them,
"sit down here, on our bench."

But the bench they offered
was a scalding stone that singed them:
they skittered and spun around.

They leapt but there was no relief,
and so they got their asses burned.

Then the Xibalban lords laughed again

      until their guts began to hurt,
      until their ribs began to ache,
      until their hearts began to cramp

as if serpents of laughter had knotted them up

and they grabbed themselves and rolled,
convulsed with laughter, all the lords of Xibalba.

"Why not just go to your hut?
We'll have someone bring

a torch and cigars there,
to your sleeping place," they told them,

and so the two of them arrived
at the House of Darkness,
where only darkness resides.

Then the Xibalban lords
gathered their thoughts and said:

"We'll sacrifice them tomorrow.
One mistake and they'll be dead

because of how we play the game,
because of our special gaming gear."

The ball they use is a globe
of blades. White Dagger
is the name of the ball of Xibalba.

The blades are honed sharp,
and pierced with shards of bone.
This is the ball they use in Xibalba.

o o o

One Hunahpu and Seven Hunahpu
entered the House of Darkness.

After a while someone arrived
with a glowing torch, already lit,

along with a pair of cigars, already lit,
sent by One Death and Seven Death.

One Hunahpu and Seven Hunahpu
hunched cross-legged in the darkness
when the torch-giver came.

He entered with the shining flame
and used it to light both cigars, saying:

"These need to be returned at dawn,
unconsumed, as they look now.

They must be collected again, intact.
This is what the lords have said."

They were told this
and thus were overthrown

for the torch burned down
as well as the cigars they were given.

Xibalba is crowded with trials.
It is a place laced with many tests.

The House of Darkness is just the first,
that place where only darkness lives.

The second one is the House of Cold.
Its rooms are coated thick with frost.
The wind howls cleanly through the door

and clatters hail against the walls.
Its whistling shrieks the emptiness.

Jaguar House is the name of the third,
where nothing but jaguars pace inside.

They slink in packs of snapping teeth,
crowding the room with fang and muscle,
moaning and gnashing their captive jaws.

The fourth trial is known as Bat House.
The interior filled with fluttering squeaks,
as they scratch, trapped, inside those walls.

Blade House is the name of the fifth:
a place where there are only blades.

They wait in alternating rows, then
flash and fall in a deadly clashing.

These are simply the names
of the houses of trial, the first
of the many tests of Xibalba.

Yet One Hunahpu and Seven Hunahpu
did not enter another

after they came from the first
and appeared before the faces
of One Death and Seven Death.

"Where are my cigars?
Where is my shining torch
that was brought to you last night?" they asked.

"We finished them, my lord."

"Then you are finished as well.
Your day is at an end.
You will die. It is time."

They were lost.
They were broken.

"Your faces will remain
hidden here forever: now
you will be sacrificed,"

said One Death and Seven Death.

They sacrificed and buried them
there at that place called
Devastation Ballcourt.

The head of One Hunahpu
was severed from his body

while his corpse was buried
there, with his younger brother.

"Take this head and put it
in the tangle of that tree
growing by the road,"

said One Death and Seven Death.

Now, when they placed his skull
into a fork in the branches,

that tree bore the first fruit
it had ever borne. No fruit

would have come without the head
of One Hunaphu planted
there, in the midst of the tangle.

This was the tree
that we now call calabash,
said to be One Hunahpu.

One Death and Seven Death
marveled at the change.

There was round fruit everywhere,
and it was no longer clear
which head belonged to One Hunahpu.

His face had grown identical
to the pale curve of the calabash.

All of Xibalba saw this
when they came out to look,

and their hearts sensed greatness
in the essence of that tree

that bore its fruit so suddenly
once the head was planted there.

Then they spoke to each other,
the Xibalbans, and they said:

"No one will ever cut this fruit,
nor enter the shade below the tree."

So the Xibalbans confined themselves:
all the Xibalbans held themselves back.

o o o

Thus, it was no longer clear
which head belonged to One Hunahpu.

His face became identical
to the pale curve of the calabash.

And so the calabash tree came to be known,
as well as the telling of this tale,
and soon a maiden heard it told:

We will tell, now, of her arrival there.

LADY BLOOD AND THE TREE OF ONE HUNAHPU

This, then, is the story of a maiden:
the daughter of the lord named Gathered Blood.
She was the daughter of a lord,
and thus was known as Lady Blood.

When she heard the account
of the fruit tree from her father,
she was astonished by the tale.

"Can't I somehow see this tree,
to better understand its strangeness?

I've heard that the fruit
is truly delicious," she said,

and she left alone to wander
beneath the calabash tree
at Devastation Ballcourt.

"Ah!
What is this fruit?

How could it not be delicious,
the fruit borne by this tree?

I will not die.
I will not be lost.

Who would even hear
if I picked one?" asked the maiden.

Then the skull spoke
there in the midst of the tree:

"What could you desire from this?
It's just bone, a round thing
stuck in the branches,"

said the head of One Hunahpu
when it spoke to the maiden.

"You do not desire it," she was told.

"But I do desire it," said the maiden.

"Then open your right hand
and reach up into the branches
so that I can see it," said the skull.

"Very well," said the maiden,
and she stretched her right hand

up to the face of the skull
and it squeezed out a little
spit into her open palm.

Then she looked into her hand—
she wasted no time, but
the skull's saliva was gone.

"The saliva was a sign
that I have given you.

This head of mine
no longer functions:
a skull without flesh
just doesn't work.

It is the same with the head
of even a great lord:
it is merely the flesh
that makes it look good

and then when he dies,
people are frightened
because of the bones.

His son remains behind,
spat into the world:
his spittle, his essence.

If his son becomes
a lord, a great sage,
a master of speech,

nothing is lost:
the line continues
to be fulfilled
and made complete.

The face of the lord
is not ruined or extinguished.
The warrior, the sage
abides in his daughters and sons.

Thus it will be so,
as I have now done to you.

Climb, then, to the face of the earth.
You will not die. You have entered

into the word. So be it," said the skull
of One Hunahpu and Seven Hunahpu.

This came from the mind,
from the thoughts of Hurricane,
Newborn Thunderbolt, and Sudden Lightning:

This was their word.

And so the maiden returned home,
having been given much instruction.

Children were created
straightaway in her womb.
They came simply from the saliva.

This, then, was the creation
of Hunahpu and Xbalanque.

Once the maiden had arrived
and spent six moons at her home,
she was found out by her father,
Gathered Blood was his name.

THE ASCENT OF LADY BLOOD FROM XIBALBA

Thus the maiden was discovered,
her father saw she was with child.

So all the lords gathered their thoughts,
One Death, Seven Death, and Gathered Blood.

"My daughter is carrying a child.
She is heavy with a bastard, my lords,"
        said Gathered Blood when the others arrived.

"Very well.

Try to pry the truth
from behind her teeth.

When she doesn't tell,
then she will be sacrificed.

We will send her far away
and she will be sacrificed."

"As you wish, my lords,"
said Gathered Blood.

Then he asked his daughter:

"Who is responsible for the child
planted in your belly, my daughter?"

"There is no child, my father.
I've yet to know the face of any man."

"But clearly you have known
something other than his face."

"Very well, warrior-lords,"
he said to the four owls.

"Sacrifice her,
and bring her heart back

here, inside this bowl, so the lords
might examine it this very day."

And so they soared into the air,
carrying the bowl and clutching
the maiden in their talons.

They took the White Dagger
as the instrument of her sacrifice.

"You messengers
will not succeed in this killing,

because what grows within me
does not come from fornication.

It was an act of mere creation.
I only went to Devastation Ballcourt
to admire the head of One Hunahpu.

Don't do this, then, you messengers.
Don't sacrifice me, please," said the maiden.

"But what can we offer
in place of your heart?

For your father said clearly:

      'Bring her heart back here,
      so the lords can examine it.

      They must hold it in their hands
      if they will be satisfied. Bring it

      quickly—place her heart
      in the hollow of this bowl.'

Is this not what we were told?
What, then, will we slip into the bowl?

For we want above all
that you should not die," said the messengers.

"Very well. Then it will be so:
my heart will not belong to them

and you will no longer make your home
here, forcing captives to their death.

You will take only those
who have truly been lascivious.

As for One Death and Seven Death
they will just receive sap

from the tree that weeps blood:
the croton tree. So be it.

This is what you will burn before them,
not this steady heart inside me.

Use what the tree gives you," she said.

The juices of the tree flowed red
and slowly drained into a bowl,
where they congealed and took shape.

The croton tree gave its pith
in place of her heart. It oozed
until it paled, offering red sap
instead of the maiden's blood.

She gathered a full bowl:
the surface glistened crimson
as she turned it in the light.

Because it was cut by the maiden
the tree is called Red Sacrifice.
She named the sap "blood,"
and blood croton it is called.

"Now you are blessed
on the face of the earth.

It has become yours,"
          she said to the owls.

"Very well, then, maiden.
We will soar upward, and hide you.

But first we must return
so that we might offer this 'heart'
before the faces of the lords,"
          said the messengers.

They arrived before the gathering
who awaited them expectantly.

"Was it not successful?" asked One Death.

"It was indeed, my lord.
Her heart is nestled here,
at the bottom of this bowl."

"Very good. Now,
let me see for myself," said One Death,

and he plucked it with his long fingers
and lifted it up into the light

so it dripped and shined with gore,
its surface bright with blood.

"Stir the face of the fire,
and place it there, above the flames," said One Death.

Then it crackled and spattered
on the fire, while all the Xibalbans
savored the fragrance.

They rose and gathered there,
leaning intently into the heat.
Hungering, as they always do,
for the delicious smell of blood.

The owls left them like this,
bent over and oblivious,
while they swept the maiden up

and left her at the opening,
there at the top of their world,
before they turned and flew back down.

So the lords of Xibalba were defeated,
because a maiden duped them blind.

LADY BLOOD AND THE MIRACLE OF MAIZE

So here is the matriarch
of One Batz and One Chouen,

and now the woman called
Lady Blood arrived before her.

She came to the matriarch,
of One Batz and One Chouen,
with her children in her womb.

But it will not be much longer
before they are born, those boys
called Hunahpu and Xbalanque.

The woman arrived and stood
before the face of the grandmother:

"I have come, my lady,
as your daughter-in-law
and as your child," she said.

"From where? From my sons?
Are they not dead, in Xibalba?

These two here are the only
mark they left behind them,
their sign and their word:

One Batz and One Chouen
are the names of the boys.

So now that you've arrived,
perhaps it's time for you to go,"
the maiden was told by the grandmother.

"But what I say is true: I am
your daughter-in-law, my lady.

What I carry inside me
belongs to him: One Hunahpu
surely gave me these children.

One Hunahpu and Seven Hunahpu
still live. They are not dead.

They have simply made a way
to come again into the light.

You will see, my mother-in-law,
when you look upon his face again

in the ones that I am carrying,"
she told the grandmother.

Now, One Batz and One Chouen
had brought light in this way:

simply through their flute and song,
through writing and carving every day,

they'd warmed the heart of their grandmother.
And so the grandmother said to her:

"I do not want you here.
You're not my daughter-in-law.

It is just your own debauchery
that is living in your womb—

you fraudulent snake!
My children are dead."

So she said again
to the grandmother:

"It is the truth that they are his!
I only speak the truth to you."

"Very well, if you are
my daughter-in-law

go then, and gather food
so these boys might eat.

Go and harvest a huge netful
of maize and drag it back here.

Then I will certainly know
you are my daughter-in-law,"
she said to the maiden.

"Very well," the maiden replied.
Then she went to the maizefield
of One Batz and One Chouen,

walking the path they had cleared
until she arrived among the maize.

Only a single ear awaited her,
there, in the field. There was
not one more, nor two, nor three.

The field had borne its maize
in a single ear on a single stalk,

and in that moment, the maiden's
heart nearly stopped and she cried:

"I owe too much.
I'm in too deep.
I am disgraced!

How will I ever get the netful
of food that's been demanded?"

So she called out to the guardians
that watch over the fields of maize:

"Come. Arise.
Come and stand,

Lady Treasurer,
Lady Golden,
Lady Cacao,
Lady Cornmeal,

you guardians
of the food
of One Batz
and One Chouen."

Then she took hold of the tassel,
the tuft of silk atop the ripened ear,

and she drew it up and plucked it out.
She did not pick the ear of maize.

Then the maize abounded.
It multiplied to swell the net
until it overflowed with food.

And thus the maiden returned.
Animals carried the net before her.

When she drew near, they returned
the pack to her and she glowed
as if she'd been the one to bear it.

The grandmother saw the great net
swollen with ripened maize and cried:

"Where did you get all this food?
Tell me, where was it stolen from?

I must go see if you have leveled
our entire field and brought it here."

Then she went to the field of maize,

and there she saw the single stalk
standing alone with its single ear

and she could clearly see the place
where the net had draped beneath.

So she said, then, to the maiden:

"This can only be a sign: truly
you are my daughter-in-law.

I must keep watching what you do,
for the grandchildren you carry
are clearly enchanted already."

HUNAHPU AND XBALANQUE IN THE HOUSE OF XMUCANE

Now, we will tell
the story of their birth,
of Hunahpu and Xbalanque.

This, then, is the account:

The day of their birth came
and Lady Blood gave birth.

Their grandmother did not see,
she was not there to witness
when they arose so suddenly,
Hunahpu and Xbalanque.

They were born in the mountains
and then came into the house
where both of them refused to sleep.

"Take them and abandon them.
Their mouths make nothing
but piercing shrieks," said the grandmother.

And so the boys were taken
and lain on the simmering anthills
where they slipped into a delicious sleep.

So they took them to the brambles
and nestled them into the thorns.

Because this was the vision
of One Batz and One Chouen:
that the boys would die out there,
among hungry ants and piercing thorns.

One Batz and One Chouen desired this
because dark treachery infected them,
they were inflamed with jealousy.

So their younger brothers
were not accepted in that house.
From the first, they were not known.

So the two boys simply grew
out among the trees and mountains.

o o o

Now, One Batz and One Chouen
were great singers and flautists.

The suffering and the misfortune
they had passed through in their lives

had given them great knowledge.
They had paid for it with pain,

becoming great singers and flautists
and writers and carvers of stone.

Everything they undertook
was gilded with great success.

They knew from where they had come
and carried that ingenious spark

standing in the place of their father
who had died, down in Xibalba.

So they were now great sages,
One Batz and One Chouen.

In their hearts they knew everything
when their younger brothers were born.

But their brilliance was blocked,
stopped up by their envy.

The abuse they plotted in their hearts
rained down on their own backs:

it went nowhere.

o o o

Hunahpu and Xbalanque
simply ignored all this.

They just took their blowguns
and hunted in the mountains.

They were not loved by their grandmother,
nor One Batz, nor One Chouen.
They were not given any food.

Once the meals were cooked,
One Batz and One Chouen
devoured them before the boys arrived.

But they did not become angry.
They did not become enflamed with rage.

They simply took it, and let it go.
They knew their own clear natures,
and they used this light to see.

Thus when the boys returned each day
bringing their birds from the hunt,

One Batz and One Chouen took them
and ate them, giving nothing to the twins.

Then they would play the flute and sing.

One day, Hunahpu and Xbalanque
returned to the hut without any birds.

Their grandmother turned red with rage:
"What is the reason for this?
Why have you not brought any birds?"

"Here's why, grandmother:
the birds are snagged
up there in the treetops.

There's no way to climb
so high into the branches
to pluck them down.

We thought, perhaps,
our older brothers could come.
They could scamper up
and fetch them down."

"Fine," said their brothers.
"We will leave at dawn."

These were the seeds of the defeat
of One Batz and One Chouen.

The twins came together
and gathered their thoughts:

"We'll simply turn their nature
back onto themselves:

the plan is born in these words
and then will come to pass
because they caused our suffering,

they abandoned us,
they wished our death—
their own little brothers!

They look on us as slaves
and make a point to work us hard.

Now we will make a point
with them," they said to each other.

So they went below the trees,
beneath the one called Yellow Tree,
accompanied by their older brothers.

They shot their blowguns as they walked.
Countless birds swarmed the treetops,
a riotous squawking flock.

Their older brothers marveled
when they saw the birds shot:
not one fell beneath the canopy.

"Our birds don't fall down here.
Just go up and fetch them,"
said the twins to their older brothers.

"Fine," they said
and clambered into the treetop.

But then the trunk thickened
and the tree began to swell
and it shot up toward the sky,
so when they wanted to come down,

One Batz and One Chouen
couldn't climb back to the ground.

They cried out from the branches:

"What can we do, little brothers?
Take pity. This tree is truly frightening."

Hunahpu and Xbalanque hollered back:

"Loosen your loincloths,
then knot it so the tail-end
dangles from your backside.

Then you'll walk more freely."

"Good," they said,

and they began to undo themselves,
pulling out the loose ends,

which unraveled into tails,
tails that suddenly curled behind

two nimble leaping monkeys,
scampering through the treetops

in the forests of the mountains,
howling and chattering raucously.

And so One Batz and One Chouen
were suddenly overthrown
by Hunahpu and Xbalanque.

It was simply the enchanted
spark inside the twins
that made it happen.

∘ ∘ ∘

Now, when they arrived back home
they spoke with their grandmother
and they spoke with their mother:

"Listen, grandmother,
something has happened
to our older brothers,

the face they show the world
is no longer so respectable.
They rave like animals now."

"If you did something
to your older brothers,

it will bring me misery,
it will bring me anguish.

Let this not be what you did
to them, my grandsons,"
said the grandmother.

"Don't grieve, grandmother.
You will certainly see the faces
of our older brothers again.

They will come back soon.
This is simply a test for you,
grandmother. So try not to laugh

while we try their destiny . . ."
and they began to play the flute.

"Hunahpu Spider Monkey"
was the name of the tune.

THE FALL OF ONE BATZ AND ONE CHOUEN

So they sang and played and drummed,

and the flute song
spun into the trees

and the drumbeat
pulsed a steady thrum.

And their grandmother
sat down beside them

while they played the tuneful music

that drifted up into the trees,
and called their names out in a song
named "Hunahpu Spider Monkey."

And they came, then,
One Batz and One Chouen:
dancing as they arrived.

When their grandmother gazed
and saw the blunt ugliness

of their faces, she burst
out into piercing laughter.

She couldn't hold back,
and they scampered away,
hiding themselves in the trees.

"What are you going to do now,
                grandmother?

We will do this four times in all,
so you only have three left.

We will draw them back again,
with the music of our flute song.

Truly, you must contain yourself.
Hold your laughter when we try again,"
said Hunahpu and Xbalanque.

So they began to play the flute,
and again they came dancing
into the clearing.

They played with great liveliness,
tempting their grandmother,
and she quickly laughed again.

The monkey-faces were truly funny,
and when they came dancing
with paunchy bellies and naked
bits that dangled from their hair,

she shook with laughter
and they fled into the mountains.

"Honestly, what will we ever
do with you, grandmother?

Now, let's try again a third time,"
said Hunahpu and Xbalanque.

They played their flutes and again
the brothers returned, dancing.

But this time their grandmother
held her laughter, and they climbed
and scampered up the walls.

Their mouths were deeply red,
their faces idiotic, puckering lips

framed in unkempt hair. Their faces
looked silly as they snorted and snuffled.

Now, when their grandmother saw this
she broke once more into rollicking laugher,
and their faces were never seen again.

"Just once more, grandmother,
we'll try to direct them back home."

And they started up their haunting tune,
but they didn't come back a fourth time.
They disappeared into the forest.

"We tried, grandmother, and at first
they came back. And we have tried
again to call them home. So,

don't be sad. We are still here,
and we are your grandsons. Just
give love to our mother, grandmother.

Our older brothers will be remembered.
                    It will be so.

They were given names,
and they were also given titles,

One Batz and One Chouen
will long be invoked,"
said Hunahpu and Xbalanque.

And since that time
they have been called upon,
flautists and singers pray to them.

The ancient ones, too, invoked their names:
those ones who wrote and carved.

      ⚬ ⚬ ⚬

They turned to animals, long ago.
They became spider monkeys
when they were swollen with pride.

For they abused their little brothers
when their hearts were overcast,
and this was their utter ruin.

Once they lost themselves,
One Batz and One Chouen,
they became only animals.

The home they dwell in now
is the hearts of flautists and singers,

for great were their deeds when they lived
with their mother and grandmother.

HUNAHPU AND XBALANQUE IN THE MAIZEFIELD

Then they began again
to reveal themselves
through their great deeds,

before the face of their grandmother,
before the face of their mother.

They started in the maizefield:

"We'll simply go
and work the fields,
dear grandmother and mother.

No need for tears or grief.
We are here. We will stand
in the place of our brothers,"
said Hunahpu and Xbalanque.

And they took up their axes,
they carried hoes on their shoulders.

They shouldered their blowguns,
as well, as they left home—but
not before telling their grandmother:

"Bring us food at high noon,
to make our midday meal."

"Very well, my grandsons,"
their grandmother replied.

They arrived at the maizefield
to clear and till the land.

They struck the hoe into the earth.
It simply plowed the earth itself.
It turned the furrow without their help.

As for the axe, they struck the blade
in the fork of a tree and it split
the wood itself. It felled the tree
with its own strength: that one axe

chopped and felled the whole tangle,
feverishly cutting bushes and trees,
while the hoe broke up thick clods
and cut down countless stalks and briars.

It roved over mountains, great and small.
That one hoe cleared them all.

Then they took a mourning dove
and placed it high upon the lone
remaining stump, and said:

"When you see our grandmother
coming to bring us our food at noon,
cry out right away and we will grasp
our hoe and our axe in our hands."

"Very well," said the mourning dove.

Then they hunted with their blowguns.
They weren't really the farming kind.

When the mourning dove cried out,
they came scampering quickly back.
One grabbed the hoe, the other the axe.

They flung field grit on their heads
and rubbed rough dirt into their hands.

One dusted his face, as if he had
truly farmed the maizefield.

The other scattered wood chips
in his hair, as if he'd cleared the trees.

This is how their grandmother
saw them when she brought their food.

They hadn't done true maize-farming
and so they hadn't earned their meal.

When they returned home, they said:
"We are truly tired, grandmother."
And they rubbed and stretched their arms
and legs, massaging them deliberately.

They went again on the following day.

When they arrived at the maizefield,
they found all the trees and bushes
risen again, all the shoots and briars
had knit themselves into a tangle.

"We got pinched and played
for fools. Who did this to us?" they said.

> Now, it was the animals
> who had done this.

> All of them,
> both great and small:

> The puma
> and the jaguar.

> The deer
> and the rabbit.

> The fox
> and the coyote.

> The peccary
> and the coati.

> The little birds
> and the big ones.

> They did it all
> in a single night.

So the twins started in again
with their maize-farming,

and again the earth was broken,
and again the trees were cut.

And they gathered their thoughts
there, among the fallen limbs
and the turned earth:

"Tonight we will come
and watch over the fields.

Whatever is happening,
we'll be sure to uncover it," they said.

Then they went back home.
"Someone is toying with us, grandmother.

When we arrived a while ago,
a great field of grass and a forest

thick with trees were growing
there, in the place of our maizefield,"

they said to their grandmother,
and their mother as well.

"So, this evening we will go
and watch over it by night.
What's been done is no good."

o o o

Thus, they concealed themselves.
They went out again to the cut trees
and hid themselves in the cover of limbs.

Meanwhile, all the animals
were gathering into one,
great and small they joined together.

They arrived in the clearing
in the dark center of night,
chattering as they came, they said:

"Arise trees, and join together.
Arise bushes. Lift yourselves."

And then they began to gather
in the shadows of the rising trees;
they emerged out of the darkness.

The puma stalked out with the jaguar
and the boys leapt to grab them

but they shook themselves free.
Then the deer and rabbit emerged,

and the boys clutched at their tails,
but they broke off at the nub

and they left them in their hands,
springing free wearing only white tufts.

And the fox and coyote shot past,
and the peccary and the coati,

they sprinted past the faces
of Hunahpu and Xbalanque,

whose hearts were churning now
because they had caught nothing.

Then one last straggler came,
scurrying pell-mell in a panic,

and in their net they caught him.
They snared themselves a rat.

They clutched him in their hands
and squeezed him hard, behind his head.

They began to strangle him
and scorched his tail over the fire

until it was naked and pink,
hairless as it is today,

his eyes still beady and desperate
from the strangling grip
of Hunahpu and Xbalanque.

"I wasn't put here to die,
and you weren't put here to farm.

Yours lies elsewhere—"
said the rat, gasping.

"Our what? Where is 'ours'?
Tell us!" said the boys.

"Will you let me go first?
The words are stuck in my belly

and I can't quite get them out.
Maybe a little food would nudge them—"

"We'll give you food later,
but you must tell us first," said the boys.

"Very well then, what is yours
was once your fathers', called

One Hunahpu and Seven Hunahpu,
who died in Xibalba.

They left behind their gaming things
tucked up in the rafters of your house:

their yoked belts and their arm-bracers,
their leathers and their rubber ball.

Your grandmother never let you see.
It was because of them your fathers died."

"Can this be true?
Do you truly know this?"

the boys asked the rat, their hearts
leaping at the news about the rubber ball.

Then they gave the rat his food.
This was the food they gave him:

grains of maize,
squash seeds,

chili peppers,
beans,

pataxte,
cacao.

"These, then,
belong to you.

If anything is swept up,
if anything is left out,

then it is yours to gnaw,"
Hunahpu and Xbalanque told the rat.

"Very well, boys,"
he answered them.

"But what will I say
if your grandmother sees?"

"Don't let your heart
turn to water now.

We are here. We know
what to tell our grandmother.

We'll lift you up into the eaves
to fetch down the things.

Go straight to where they're hanging.
We'll be able to see you in the rafters

while we are looking down
at the reflection in our bowls.

We'll see you in the surface
of our broth," they told the rat.

So Hunahpu and Xbalanque
gathered their thoughts,
instructing the rat all night.

They arrived home the next day
when the sun was at its peak.

HUNAHPU AND XBALANQUE DISCOVER
THE GAMING THINGS

The rat was tucked away,
well hidden, when they arrived.

One went straight into the house,
while the other darted round the corner
and placed the rat up into the rafters.

Then they asked their grandmother
for a bowl of food: "Just mash a bite
to eat. Perhaps a bowl of chili broth."

So their bite was prepared,
and the bowl was placed before them.

This is how they toyed with them,
their grandmother and mother:
they drained the water jug dry.

"Our mouths are truly parched.
Can you bring us a drink?"

they asked their grandmother,
and she left, leaving them to eat.

But they weren't even hungry,
they just played out their ruse,

watching the rat reflected
in the surface of the broth

until he settled behind the rubber ball
hanging there, above the house.

Then they sent out a mosquito,
that whining cousin to the biting fly.

It went down to the river and
pierced the face of the water jug,

so whenever she scooped water,
it came leaking from the jug.

Try as she might, she could not
seal the face of that leaky vessel.

"What on earth is she doing,
that grandmother of ours?

We are gasping with thirst!
Our mouths are dry as sand,"

they said to their mother,
and they sent her to the river.

Then the rat went to work,
clawing at the knotted tethers

until the rubber ball fell
bouncing from the thatch,

along with the yoked-belts,
leathers, and arm-bracers.

The twins ran to hide them,
along the road to the ballcourt,

then they walked to the river,
to where their mother was trying,

along with their grandmother,
to keep the face of the jug from weeping.

They arrived there, at the river,
with their blowguns on their shoulders.

"What have you been doing?
Our hearts got tired of waiting,
so we came," said the boys.

"Look at the face of this jug.
It cannot be sealed up," said their grandmother.

So the boys stopped it up,
and they came home again,
leading the way for their grandmother.

This was the discovery of the rubber ball.

THE SUMMONS OF HUNAHPU AND XBALANQUE
TO XIBALBA

And so the boys rejoiced: they went
as ballplayers to the ballcourt.

They swept out the court
of their fathers,

and for a long time,
they played ball there, alone.

Then they heard it from below,
those lords of Xibalba: '

"Someone's started the game again,
up there, above our heads.

Have they no shame,
stomping on our roof?

Didn't they die?
One Hunahpu and Seven Hunahpu?
When they desired to show us up?

Go summon these players, then,"
said the lords once more,

said One Death and Seven Death,
and all the other lords.

"Summon them here,"
they said to the messengers.
"Say to them when you arrive:

     'The lords have proclaimed:
         You must come!

         We wish you to come
         and play ball with us.

         In seven days
         we will play,

         said the lords.'

Tell them this when you arrive,"
said the lords to the messengers.
And so they came, soaring
over the great cleared pathway,
over the road to the boys' home.

They swooped into the house,
the messengers of Xibalba,

alighting in the house of the grandmother
while the boys were out playing ball.

"The lords have said:
         They must surely come,"

said the messengers of Xibalba.

Then they specified the date:
"In seven days, they are expected,"
the messengers told Xmucane.

"Very well, you messengers,
they will go as summoned,"
          said the grandmother.

And the messengers returned,
quick as they came, leaving
the grandmother heartsick:

"How will I tell my grandsons
of this summons?

Were these not
truly Xibalbans?

They are just like those
messengers that came before,

when their fathers
went off to die,"

said the grandmother,
streaming tears in her house, alone.

Then, a louse dropped onto her.

It itched and so she plucked it
and put it in her palm.

It scuttled sideways as it
walked about her hand.

"Oh, my grandchild,"
she said to the louse.

"Would you like me
to send you to the ballcourt
to fetch my grandsons?"

So the louse crept away
bearing this message:

"Messengers came to your grandmother.
        They say that you must come.
        You must come in seven days,
            said the messengers of Xibalba.
This is what your grandmother says."

The louse crawled along,
scuttling through the dust,

until he came upon a sleek toad
sitting in the path, named Tamazul.

"Where are you going?" asked the toad.

"I'm taking this burden,
these words in my belly,

to the boys at the ballcourt,"
said the louse to Tamazul.

"Very well then.
But I see you're not going

particularly fast,"
said the toad to the louse.

"Wouldn't you like me
to swallow you?

Then you'd see how fast I go.
We'd get there quickly."

"Sounds good," said the louse,

and the toad licked him up
and went hopping down the road.
So there he goes, now,
flopping along,
but he's not too swift

and so then he was met
by a great whitesnake,
named Zaquicaz.

"Where are you going,
Tamazul, my boy?"
the snake asked the toad.

"I'm a messenger.
My word is down there,
in my belly," replied the toad.

"You're not so quick, I see.
Perhaps I'd get there faster?"

"Be my guest," said the toad
and he was swallowed in one gulp.

The snake, then, got his food.
They still eat toads in just this way.

Now, the snake went winding
quickly down the road,

until he was spied by a falcon,
hovering on great wings,

and the snake was swallowed up
like a loose piece of rope.

The falcon lifted away
and perched above the ballcourt,

and so they both arrived,
and falcons still eat snakes today.

The falcon perched on the stone wall
rimming the top of the ballcourt

while Hunahupu and Xbalanque
rejoiced below, playing ball.

The falcon arrived and gave
its piercing cry: "Wak-ko! Wak-ko!"

"What is this, crying out?
Let's grab our blowguns!" said the twins.

And so they shot the falcon,
they buried a pellet deep in its eye,

and he was knocked from his perch,
crumpling down to the ground.

They ran to seize and question him.
"Why have you come?" they asked.

"The words are lodged in my belly.
Once you cure my eye, I will tell,"
                              said the falcon.

"Very well," they replied,
and they shaved away the surface

of the rubber ball and put it there,
as a patch over the bird's eye,

sacrificing a bit of that vital sap,
and straightaway he was cured:

his sight became good again.
"Now, spit those words out,"
they said to the falcon.

So he vomited up the writhing snake.
"Cough it up," they said to the snake.

"Fine," he said, and vomited the toad.

"What is your errand? Share it,"
they then told the toad.

"The words are here in my belly,"
said the toad, as he tried to puke.

But he wasn't able to vomit.
He just sort of drooled a little.

He tried again, but the heave was dry,
and the boys yearned to pummel him.

"You're a liar," they told him,
and they squashed his rear end,

crushing the bones of his backside
as they mashed down their feet.

Again he tried: nothing but spit.

Then the mouth of the toad
was pried open by the boys.

They searched and found the louse
pasted on the front of his gums.

The toad hadn't swallowed him
at all: it merely seemed that way.

So the toad was defeated,
and no one knows what food he eats.

He drags his backside, hopping,
and to this day is food for snakes.

"Speak," the louse was told again,
and so he spoke his word:

"Your grandmother says to you:

       'Go now, and summon those boys
       for others have come to summon them.

       The messengers came from Xibalba,
       from One Death and Seven Death, saying:

              "'In seven days
              they will arrive
              and we'll play ball.

              Tell them to bring
              their gaming things:

their belts and leathers,
and their arm-bracers,
and their steady rubber ball.

They will liven things up
down here,' said the lords."

This is what they said.
So now you must come.'

This is what your grandmother said.
Now she is weeping and crying out
that you must come," said the louse.

"Can this be true?" said the boys.
They looked into their hearts
when they heard these words,

then returned home straightaway
to advise their grandmother.

THE DESCENT OF HUNAHPU AND XBALANQUE INTO XIBALBA

"We must go, grandmother,
but we will advise you first.

This, then, is our sign.
This, then, is our word
that we will leave behind:

Each of us will plant an ear
of unripe maize, here in the floor
in the center of our house.

If they dry and wither
you will know we have died.

'They have died,' you will say
when the ears have dried up.

If then they send out
green sprouts once again,

'They are alive,' you will say,
our grandmother and mother.

Do not weep, then. For this
is now our sign and our word.
It will remain behind with you," they said.

Then each went and planted one,
Hunahpu and Xbalanque.
They simply dug into the floor.

They did not go to the mountains.
They did not seek out fertile ground.

They simply planted them,
there, in the dry packed earth
in the center of their hut.

Then they departed,
shouldering their blowguns,
and descended to Xibalba.

They went straight down the steps
passing into the various canyons.

They passed through
circling throngs of birds,
the ones that swarm in flocks.

They passed again over the river
of pus, the river dark with blood,
places the Xibalbans meant as traps.

But the twins were untroubled.
They simply floated on their blowguns.

Then they arrived again
where the four roads crossed,

and they already knew
the roads of Xibalba—

black road, white road,
red road, and yellow road—

and from that place
they sent out a listener,

an insect named Mosquito,
to obtain what he might hear.

"You will bite them all in turn.
Begin with the one who sits

in the first seat, then keep
biting to the very last.

This will be your gift:
to suck the blood of travelers,"
the boys told the mosquito.

"Very well," said the mosquito,
and flew away down the black road.

◦ ◦ ◦

He alighted behind them:
the figures carved from wood.

The one seated first
was very well dressed,

and so he bit him,
but he did not speak.

Then he bit the one
sitting in the second seat,

and he was silent as well.
Then he bit the one

sitting in the third seat,
who was One Death.

All the lords cried "Ouch!"
when they were bitten.

It went just like this:

> "Ow!" said One Death.

> "What, One Death? What is it?"

> "I just got bit!"

> "It's only—Ow! What is that?
> Now I'm being bitten!"
> said the one seated fourth.

> "What, Seven Death? What is it?"

> "I just got bit!"

Then the one seated fifth
said, "Ow! Ow!"

"Flying Scab, what is it?" asked Seven Death.

"Now I'm getting bit!"

Then the one seated sixth
hollered, "Ouch!"

"What, Gathered Blood? What is it?"
asked Flying Scab.

"I just got bit," he said.

Then the one seated seventh
was bitten, and cried, "Ow!"

"What, Pus Demon? What is it?"
asked Gathered Blood.

"I just got bit," he said.

Then the one seated eighth
was bitten: he was the next to say:

"Ow!"

"What, Jaundice Fiend? What is it?"
asked Pus Demon.

"I just got bit," he said.

Then the one seated ninth
was bitten, and cried, "Ow!"

"What, Bone Lance? What is it?"
asked Jaundice Fiend.

"I just got bit," he said.

Then the one seated tenth
was bitten, and cried, "Ow!"

"What, Skull Staff? What is it?"
asked Bone Lance.

"I just got bit," he said.

Then the one seated eleventh
was bitten, and cried, "Ow!"

"What, Wingspan? What is it?"
asked Skull Staff.

"I just got bit," he said.

Then the one seated twelfth
was bitten, and cried, "Ow!"

"What, Packstrap? What is it?"
asked Wingspan.

"I just got bit," he said.

Then the one seated thirteenth
was bitten, and cried, "Ow!"

"What, Bloody Teeth? What is it?"
asked Packstrap.

"I just got bit," he said.

Then the one seated fourteenth
was bitten, and cried, "Ow!"

"What, Bloody Claws? What is it?"
asked Bloody Teeth.

"I just got bit," he said.

So all their names were named.

Each one called the name of another,
and each was named in rank and order
by the lord who sat there, at his side.

Not a single one was missed.
All of them were now revealed
just because they felt the bite

       of a single hair plucked
       from Hunahpu's knee:

it wasn't even really a mosquito
that went to gather all those names
for Hunahpu and Xbalanque.

◦ ◦ ◦

They arrived, then,
among the lords of Xibalba.

"Hail these lords, seated here!"
called out a voice to tempt them.

"They are not lords,
these puppets seated here.

They are merely figures
carved from wood,"
said the twins as they arrived.

And they called out to hail them all:

> "Good morning, One Death.
> Good morning, Seven Death.
>
> Good morning, Flying Scab.
> Good morning, Gathered Blood.
>
> Good morning, Pus Demon.
> Good morning, Jaundice Fiend.

Good morning, Bone Lance.
Good morning, Skull Staff.

Good morning, Wingspan.
Good morning, Packstrap.

Good morning, Bloody Teeth.
Good morning, Bloody Claws."

And so the faces of all the lords
were reflected back to them.

The twins named every name.
Not a single one was missed.

When the moment demanded,
they revealed the face of every lord.

"Have a seat," they were told.

The lords offered them a bench,
but they were not inclined to take it:

"This isn't the bench for us.
It's just a heated cooking slab,"

said Hunahupu and Xbalanque.
Thus they were not undone.

"Fine. Just go in that house, then,"
the boys were told, and they went
into the House of Darkness.

Nor were they overthrown there,
in that first trial of Xibalba,
even though the Xibalban lords
had decreed it in their hearts.

So they entered the House of Darkness:

After a while someone arrived,
with a glowing torch, already lit,
as well as cigars for each of them.

The messenger from One Death said:

"The lord says:
>   'This is their torch.
>   It must be returned
>
>   again, at dawn,
>   along with these cigars.
>
>   They must be returned
>   again, intact.'"

"Very well," said the twins.

But they didn't light the torch.
They covered it with the scarlet
gleam of a macaw's tail feather,

and all night long the watchmen
watched it flash and glimmer.

As for the cigars, they simply
tucked fireflies into their tips.

They pulsed and glowed,
lighting up the dark night,

and the watchmen said:
"We have defeated them."

But the torch was not
consumed by the illusion.

The cigars were not
burnt in the least.

The following morning
they returned everything whole
to the lords, who said:

"How is it they became like this?
Where did these two come from?

Who was the one who bore these children?
Who was the one who planted them?

Our hearts are truly troubled;
it's devious what they are doing to us.

Their appearance is utterly different,
and their essence is distinctive."

So the lords murmured, gathered together,
and then they summoned them:

"Let's play ball, boys,"

said One Death and Seven Death,
and then they questioned them.

"Where exactly do you come from, boys?
Won't you name the place?"

"We must have come from somewhere
but we don't know where that is."

They said only that,
and so told nothing.

"Very well.
Let's just go play ball, boys,"
said the lords of Xibalba.

"Fine," said the boys.

"Here is the rubber ball we'll use,"
said the Xibalbans.

"No, let's use ours," said the boys.

"No. We'll use this one. Ours,"
repeated the Xibalbans.

"Fine," said the boys.

"It only looks like a skull.
That's just a drawing on the ball,"
said the Xibalbans.

"That's not a drawing," said the boys.
"We say that's a skull."

"It is not," said the Xibalbans.

"Very good, then," said Hunahpu.

Then the Xibalbans
threw down their ball and it

landed before Hunahpu,
and as the Xibalbans looked on,

the White Dagger
burst from inside the ball.

It came spinning and slashing,
knifing the length of the ballcourt.

"What is this?"
asked Hunahpu and Xbalanque.

"Death is the only thing
you wish for us.

Didn't we answer your summons?
Weren't those your messengers that came?

Truly, have some pity
or we'll just leave,"
said the boys to the lords.

Now, the lords had hoped
the boys would already be dead,
sliced to bits by the blade,

but it was not so.
Once again, the Xibalbans
had been outdone by the boys.

"Don't go, boys. Let's play ball,
truly. We'll just use yours,"
said the lords to the twins.

"Very well," they replied.

And so their steady rubber ball
was dropped onto the court.

Then they chose the prizes:

"What will we win?" asked the Xibalbans.

"Whatever you choose, clearly," said the boys.

"We'll simply take four bowls
of flowers. That will be our cut," said the Xibalbans.

"Very well," said the boys. "What kind?"

"One bowl filled with red petals,
one bowl filled with white petals,
one bowl filled with yellow petals,
and one bowl brimming with large ones," said the Xibalbans.

"Very well," said the boys.

Then the ball was dropped:

Their strength was evenly matched.
Many deft plays were made by the boys,
drawing deep from their good hearts.

When, finally, the twins succumbed,
the Xibalbans rejoiced at their defeat:

"We have done well.
We defeated them in the first try,"
said the Xibalbans aloud.

"Where will they ever go
to get those flowers?"
they wondered in their hearts.

"You can bring us our prize,
those flowers, very early in the morning,"
said the lords to Hunahpu and Xbalanque.

"Very well.
Then we'll play ball again
first thing in the morning,"
said the twins, conferring with one another.

Then they went to Blade House,
the second trial of Xibalba,
and entered to spend the night.

They were to be sliced open
by knives there, cut apart
into chunks. It was to happen

quick as flashing light, but it
did not turn out that way.

They spoke to the blades,
instructing them in this way:

"This will be yours: the flesh
of all animals," said the boys.

And the blades stilled.
They did not move again
other than to lower their points, as one.

Then while the boys were passing
the night, there, in Blade House,
they called out to the ants:

"Leafcutters, conquering ants, come!

All of you must go
to cut the blossoms for us,
to fetch the prizes of the lords."

"Very well," said the ants.

So the ants went to get flowers
from the garden of One Death and Seven Death.

Now, the lords of Xibalba
had already instructed
the guardians of their flowers:

"Look after the blooms.
Be vigilant. Do not allow
even one to be cadged.

For by these blossoms,
we have defeated those boys.

What if they came upon
these blooms as our prize?
There is not one of you
that will sleep tonight," they said.

"Very well," said the guardians.

But the guardians of the garden
noticed nothing. They cried out

aimlessly in the branches above,
and toddled the garden paths as well,
endlessly repeating their song:

"Shpurpuwek, Shpurpuwek,"
says one as he calls.

"Puhuyu, Puhuyu,"
says the other in answer.

These two whippoorwills
were the guardians of the garden
of One Death and Seven Death.

They never sensed those ants
were stealing what they were guarding.

The ants boiled up in a throng
of simmering black lines, carrying petals

they had cut from the treetops
and petals gathered from beneath the limbs.

All this was done while the guardians
called to one another, oblivious

that their tails and wings
were being snipped away as well.

Thus the blossoms were loosened
and fell to be gathered

and quickly filled four bowls with petals.
By dawn, they were brimming full.

∘ ∘ ∘

The messengers arrived to summon them.
        "'Come' says the lord.
        'Bring us our prize
        straightaway!'"
This is what the boys were told.

"Very well," they said,
for there were the four bowls
of blossoms they had gathered.

They went and arrived
before the faces of the lords,

who received the flowers
exchanging woeful looks.

Thus the Xibalbans were undone,
by mere ants sent by boys,

who spent the whole night
steadily filling those bowls.

The faces of the Xibalbans
drained completely white,
they went pallid because of those petals.

Then they summoned the guardians:

"What reason can you give
for our flowers being stolen?

These flowers we are offered
are ours!" they told the guardians.

"We didn't notice anything, my lord,
but our tails surely suffered for it," they replied.

Then their mouths were cracked open
for allowing those blooms to be stolen,

and One Death and Seven Death
were undone by Hunahpu and Xbalanque.

This is why whippoorwills
gape open their mouths, crying
the same cry to this very day.

          o o o

Then once again the ball was dropped,
and the game came out dead-even.

When it was done, they came together:

"Tomorrow, at dawn," said the Xibalbans.

"Very well," said the twins, once they were done.

HUNAHPU AND XBALANQUE IN THE HOUSE OF COLD

So they entered into the House of Cold
where the cold is immeasurable,

and the rooms clatter with hail
in the place cold calls home.

But sudden as they came inside
the cold melted into nothingness.

They thawed the chill, they ruined
and shattered that cold, those boys.

So they didn't die, but glowed
with life when the dawn came.

They stymied the Xibalbans
who had hoped for frozen death.

But no. Those boys raised
their faces when dawn came,

along with the messengers,
to summon them again.

"What is this? They're not dead?"
said the lords of Xibalba.

And again they marveled
at the deeds of the twins, of Hunahpu and Xbalanque.

HUNAHPU AND XBALANQUE IN JAGUAR HOUSE

So next they entered Jaguar House,
crowded thick with jaguars.

"No need to eat us. What is yours
is right here," they told the jaguars,

scattering bones before the beasts,
who bolted them, voraciously.

The bones splintered and cracked
and the night watchmen found this

crunching sweet, saying, "Finally,
they are finished. The jaguars devoured

their hearts and now they crunch
their skeletons into shards."

But their faces looked just fine
when they walked out of Jaguar House.

"What kind of people are they?
Where on earth have they come from?"
                    asked all of the Xibalbans.

HUNAHPU AND XBALANQUE IN THE HOUSE OF FIRE

Next they went into the fire,
a house where only fire lives.

It holds only crackling flames,
but they were not burned.

They went there to be roasted,
to be burnt down to blackened cinders.

But they looked just fine at dawn.
Sudden flaming death was the wish,

but no: they passed through,
and the Xibalbans lost heart because of it.

HUNAHPU AND XBALANQUE IN BAT HOUSE

Next they were put into Bat House,
where there is nothing but shrieking bats:

a house filled with huge wings
and murderous beasts.

Their snouts slash like knives:
this is the method of their killing.

The twins were meant to meet their end
as soon as they walked inside,

but they crawled inside their blowguns
and that is where they went to sleep.

They were not eaten by those beasts
swooping through the house.

Still, a single death-bat did them in.
It descended, dropping like a blade.

But this only allowed the twins
to show the luminous spirit inside them.

° ° °

They were pleading hard for wisdom,
as bat-wings shuffled the air,

shrieking "Keeleetz! Keeleetz!"
all through the black night,

until finally things grew quiet
and the restless wings fell still.

Xbalanque crawled to the end
of his blowgun, and called:

"Hunahpu, has it begun to dawn?"
"I'll go see for certain if it's come,"

said Hunahpu, crawling to the mouth
of his blowgun to look for the light.

And as his head peered out,
it was lopped off by a death-bat,
leaving the hulk of his body behind.

"What? Hasn't it dawned yet?"
asked Xbalanque.

But Hunahpu lay motionless.

"What's going on? Hunahpu?
He wouldn't have left.
What has he done?"

But nothing moved. There was
only the slightest rustle of wings.

Xbalanque was crestfallen: "Alas,
we have given it up, already."

° ° °

At the word of One Death and Seven Death,
the head was stuck on a pike
atop the wall that rimmed the ballcourt.

All the Xibalbans rejoiced to see it,
the head of Hunahpu.

In the meantime, Xbalanque
had summoned all the animals:

> Coati and Peccary,
> all the small animals,
> and all the big ones

while it was still very dark,
on the brink of early morning.

Then he asked them to bring food:
"Whatever it is that each of you eats,
I ask you to gather it here," said Xbalanque.

"Very well," said the animals,
and they went to get what was theirs,
and then all of them returned.

Some of them brought rotten things.
Some of them just brought back leaves.

Some of them just brought back stones.
Some of them just brought back dirt.

And so the animals, great and small,
brought back all the things they eat,

until the coati came straggling,
bringing a chilacayote squash,
nudging and rolling it with her nose.

This would be the thing that changed
into the head of Hunahpu.

Right away they carved out eyes.
The sky sent down a crowd of sages:

Heart of Sky, known as Hurricane,
appeared there, in the Bat House.

It didn't happen any too soon,
that they got his new head straight:

His face was handsome as ever,
and he could even speak a little,

but Hunahpu's face was not done
when the roots of the sky grew red,

when they looked to the horizon
and saw that it wanted to dawn.

"Blacken it up with soot again, old man,"
the possum was told.

"Fine," said that grey-haired grandfather,
and he blackened the sky with soot
until once again it was dark as night.

Four times that grandfather
blackened the sky with soot.

Some people still say today
that possum streaks the sky at dawn,

so it turns red before it grows blue
just as when it began its existence.

"Isn't it good?" they asked Hunahpu.

"Yes, very good," he answered.

His head sat sturdy on his neck
and came to be good as his true one.

Then the twins went into council.
They wove their words into a ruse:

"Don't play any ball quite yet.
Just stand tall and look tough.
I'll be the one to make this happen,"
said Xbalanque to Hunahpu.

And then he instructed a rabbit:

> "Settle yourself, there,
> at the head of the ballcourt.
> Nestle in the tomato patch,"

said Xbalanque to the rabbit.

> "When the ball comes your way
> leap out and sprint away
> until my work is done."

So the rabbit received
his instructions from the twins
there in the dark,

and when it finally dawned,
both their faces looked just fine.

THE HEAD OF HUNAHPU RESTORED

So once again
the game began

and a new ball
was put into play:

the head of Hunahpu
was rolled onto the court.

> "You're good
> as dead.

> Already,
> we've won.

> You lost
> your head

> and now
> you're done,"

said the Xibalbans.

But Hunahpu just hollered:
"Why not punt that head
as if it were a ball?"

"They can't harm us.
We'll be the ones to threaten them,"
cried the Xibalban lords
as they struck the ball into play.

Xbalanque met it with his
yoked-belt and sent it flying

straight out of the ballcourt,
bouncing once, then twice

until it rolled into the tomatoes
and the rabbit burst out, frantic

and leaping as the Xibalbans
gave chase, shouting all the while.

All the Xibalbans fled after him,
and the twins retrieved the head

of Hunahpu from the tomatoes,
and they planted it back onto his neck
where once the squash had been.

Then they returned to the ballcourt,
carrying the chilacayote squash,

while the true head of Hunahpu
smiled and rejoiced with Xbalanque.

The Xibalbans were out chasing,
still searching for their ball,

when the twins called to them:
"Come on! We found the ball!"

The twins were holding the round "ball"
when the Xibalbans returned and asked:

"What just happened?
What exactly did we just see?"

Then they began
to play ball again.

The game was balanced.
They played dead-even

until at last Xbalanque
struck the chilacayote

and it squashed open
to scatter its seeds
before their startled faces.

"What is this thing?
Who brought it?"
said the Xibalbans.

And with this,
those lords were defeated
by Hunahpu and Xbalanque.

They passed through this
danger and did not die,
though everything was done to them.

THE DEATH OF HUNAHPU AND XBALANQUE

This, then, is the account:
the memorial of the deaths
of Hunahpu and Xbalanque.

We will tell it now
in memory of them.

They did what they planned,
despite all the affliction

and despite all the torment
that was sprung upon them.

They did not die
in the many trials of Xibalba.

Nor were they devoured
by the ravenous beasts lurking there.

Then the time came
to summon two seers.
They were true sages,

visionaries named
Descent and Ascent,

or Xulu and Paqam,
as they are known:

"The lords of Xibalba might come
and inquire about our deaths.

Even now they are gathering
their thoughts, because we have yet
to die, nor have we been defeated.

We confounded their trials.
We eluded the hungry animals.
Yet still this sign has come to our hearts:

We will be killed by heated stones.
Ovens will be the means of our murder.

All the Xibalbans have gathered:
How can we not die forever?
These, then, will be your thoughts,
what we are telling you now,

should you come to be asked by them
about our deaths once we are burned.

So what should you tell them,
you Xulu, and you Paqam, if they ask:

'Wouldn't it perhaps be good
if we scattered their bones in the canyon?'

Say: 'Perhaps not. They would simply
arise and lift their faces to the light.'

And if they ask: 'Would it be better
to simply hang them in the treetops?'

Say: 'Certainly not, unless you wish
to always see their faces before you.'

Then the third time, when they ask:
'Perhaps it might be the best thing

to simply scatter their bones
over the course of the river?'

Say: 'It is good that they die.
And it would be good, too,

to grind their bones down to flour
on the face of a grinding stone,

until they are ground fine as maize.
Then scatter this over the flowing river,

sprinkle it into that water that winds
through the mountains, great and small.'

This, then, is what you will say.
And it will be revealed, just so,

what we have said to you in counsel now,"
said little Hunahpu and Xbalanque.

When they spoke these words,
they already knew their death was coming.

For even then the Xibalbans
were heating up the huge stones

in the pit oven they had dug,
the place for roasting meat.

They filled it with large coals,
glimmering with red flame.

And then the messengers arrived
from One Death and Seven Death
to accompany the twins, saying:

"The lords told us:

> 'Go and bring those boys!
> Let them come and see
> what we have cooked up now!'

This is what the lords have said."

"Very well," said the twins,
and they went straightaway,

arriving at the mouth of the pit
where the Xibalbans wished
to force them into playing a game:

"Let's jump over this pit
where we're brewing our sweet drink.

Four times we'll cross it,
each one of us," said One Death.

"We won't be playing,"
said the twins.
"Nor will you play us

for fools! Do you think
we cannot recognize

death when we see it?
Here, let us show you!"

and then they faced one another,
and clasped their hands together,
and dove headfirst into the oven.

So both of them died there,
and all of Xibalba rejoiced.

Contented shouts rang out,
contented whistles as well.

"It sure took a while
but we defeated them, at last!"

And then the lords summoned
Xulu and Paqam,

who carried the words
the boys left behind.

The Xibalbans consulted
and once they had divined it,

they took care of those bones:
they ground them up fine

and sprinkled them along the river
where they sank into the water.

o o o

Chosen boys, they came to be,
when their faces appeared
growing from those bits of bone.

THE RESURRECTION OF HUNAHPU
AND XBALANQUE

On the fifth day they appeared again.
People saw them on the river bottom,
looking like some kind of human-fish.

When the Xibalbans saw those faces,
they looked for them in the rivers.

So the next day, two orphans
appeared in nothing but tatters:

>   rags on their fronts,
>   rags on their backs,
>   rags were all that covered them.

But they did not act as expected
when they were seen by Xibalba,
for now they only danced:

>   the dance of the Whippoorwill,
>   and the dance of the Weasel,
>   and the dance of the Armadillo.

They danced the Centipede,
while walking on stilts,
and they danced with daggers
swallowed down their throats.

They did many marvelous things:

they set fire to a house
so it was truly burning

then quick as a flash
made it whole again.

All of the Xibalbans
crowded around to watch.

Then they sacrificed themselves:
one of the twins would die,
stretched out dead as a stone.

Then once he was killed,
his face would revive
and glow with life.

The Xibalbans simply watched
with admiration as they did these deeds,

while the twins laid the groundwork
for the defeat of Xibalba at their hands.

THE SUMMONS OF HUNAHPU AND XBALANQUE
BEFORE THE LORDS

Soon the news of their dances
reached One Death and Seven Death,
and they said to one another:

"Who are these ragged orphans?
Are they truly this delightful?

Can it truly be so beautiful,
their dancing and their marvels?"

The lords were delighted
by all the accounts that arrived,

so they entreated their messengers
to summon these two boys:

"You will say,

        'If they would only come
        so we can see them dance,

        we would certainly marvel
        and wonder as we watch,'"

so the messengers were told.

Then they went to the dancers,
and repeated what the lords had said.

"We do not want to go!
In truth, we are timid.

We would be ashamed
to enter such a lordly house,

staring with our ugly faces,
wide-eyed in our poverty.

Can't they see we're just dancers?

What would we say
to all our fellow orphans?

They depend upon us
to brighten their faces
with our dancing;

it is not fitting
that we should do the same
with these lords.

So, messengers,
we simply don't want to,"
			said Hunahpu and Xbalanque.

But they were pestered
and they were threatened
by misfortune and pain,

and so they went,
dragging their feet
in apprehension.

They were surely in no hurry:
the messengers prodded them

as they made their slow progress,
as they were taken back to the lords.

HUNAHPU AND XBALANQUE DANCE BEFORE THE LORDS OF XIBALBA

When they arrived there,
before the lords, they made
an elaborate show of being humble.

Prostrating themselves,
stooping and bowing,

concealing their faces
among their tattered rags:
they truly looked like orphans.

Then the lords asked them
what mountain they called home,

and who they called their people,
their mother and their father.

"Where do you come from?"
                 they were asked.

"We do not know, my lord.
We never learned the faces
of our mother and father,

we were still so small
when they both died."

This was all they said,
and so said nothing at all.

"Very well, then.
Now, on with the spectacle!
What do you wish as payment?"

"We do not want anything.
To tell the truth, we are afraid,"
said the twins to the lords.

"Do not be afraid.
Do not be timid. Just dance!

First you will do your dancing,
then you will sacrifice yourselves,
then you will burn our home.

Do all the things you know.
This is why you were summoned here.
Deep in our hearts we wish to watch,

and because you are poor orphans
we will pay any price you wish,"
said the Xibalbans to the boys.

So they began to play their songs
and stepped into their dances,

and all the Xibalbans came streaming,
until the hall was overflowing,
and everything was danced:

They danced the Weasel.
They danced the Whippoorwill.
They danced the Armadillo.

Then the lord spoke to them:

"Sacrifice my dog, and then
revive him once again—"

"All right," said the boys,
and so they sacrificed the dog,
and revived him once again,

and the dog was truly happy
when they brought him back to life,

he nuzzled them and wagged his tail
once he had been revived.

Then the lord spoke to them again:

"Now you must burn my home!"

And so they burned
the home of the lord,

that house overflowing
with countless Xibalbans,
and not one of them was singed.

Immediately, it was restored,
lest One Death lose his home

too soon, and all the lords marveled.
The boys were simply dancing,
while the lords erupted in rejoicing.

Then next they were told by the lord:

"Kill somebody! Any person!
Sacrifice him! But so he doesn't die—"

"Fine," said the boys, and they
seized a person and sacrificed him.

They cut the heart out of the body
and held it up before the faces of the lords.

Now, One Death and Seven Death
began to truly marvel, for immediately
the face of the man was revived,

and his heart was filled with joy
when he came back to life,
and the lords were filled with wonder:

"Now, sacrifice yourselves.
We want to see it! Truly, you are
dancing the desire of our hearts!"
                    said all of the lords.

"Very well," the boys replied.

So then they sacrificed themselves:
Hunahpu was killed by Xbalanque.

He was cut into pieces,
arms and legs severed, head
lopped off and rolled far away.

His heart was dug out
and wrapped up in a leaf,

and the lords of Xibalba
were crazed at the sight,
drunk on their hunger,

as Xblanque danced, alone.

"Arise!" he said, and immediately
Hunahpu revived again,

and the lords began rejoicing.

One Death and Seven Death
rejoiced in their hearts,
as if they'd done it themselves,

as if they'd entered and felt
the pulse of the dance.

THE DEFEAT OF THE LORDS OF XIBALBA

Now, it was the lords' desire
to abandon their hearts to the dance
of Hunahpu and Xbalanque.

Then came the words
of One Death and Seven Death.

"Do it to us! Sacrifice us!
Do it the same way, at last!"

cried One Death and Seven Death
to Hunahpu and Xbalanque.

"Very well.
Surely you will be revived.
What is death to death itself?

We are only here to gladden you,
as well as your servants and minions,"
said the twins to the lords.

The first to be sacrificed
was the very head of the lords,
One Death by name, Lord of Xibalba.

So now he was dead, this One Death,
and then they took Seven Death,
and neither one came back to life.

All the Xibalbans
leapt to their feet and fled

once they saw their lords
were dead and being torn open,

their hearts ripped from their chests
as punishment for all they'd done.

The first lord was executed
straightaway and not revived,

but the other lord began to grovel
and weep before the dancers, unable
to accept the place he'd found himself:

"Pity me," he said, too late.

All the lesser lords and servants
fled into the canyons,

the whole herd of them stuffed
into one ravine, piled
one on top of the other,

and countless ants gathered
and swarmed into the canyons,
as if they had been driven there,

and as the ants arrived, seething,
the Xibalbans bowed down
and gave themselves up.

They approached,
begging and weeping,
utterly humbled.

Thus were defeated
all the lords of Xibalba.

o o o

It was simply a miracle:
the boys transformed
themselves when they did it.

Then they declared their names.
They revealed themselves
before all of Xibalba.

THE MIRACULOUS MAIZE OF HUNAHPU
AND XBALANQUE

"Hear our names!

We will name our names now,
and we will also declare
the names of our fathers.

Here we are: little
Hunahpu and Xbalanque.

And these are our fathers,
the ones you killed:

One Hunahpu
and Seven Hunahpu.

We come to avenge
their misfortune and affliction,

and for this reason we endured
all your pain and tribulation.

And now we will destroy you.
All of you. We will kill you.

There is not one who will be saved,"
        so they told the Xibalbans,

and all of Xibalba fell to begging
and weeping: "Take pity on us,

Hunahpu and Xbalanque.
It is true we wronged your fathers,

the ones you named, the ones
buried at Devastation Ballcourt,"
                                    they said.

"Very well.

This, then, is our word
we say to you.

Hear it now,
all you Xibalbans:

Your day has passed.

Never again will you
or your offspring
lord over all.

Your offerings
will be diminished

to croton sap
and unclean blood,

already spent,
already spilled,

to battered stoves
and worn-out pots,

to what no longer
holds its shape

to what is brittle
and easily broken.

You will eat only
what roams the meadows,
what roams the wastelands.

None of the children
born and bred in the light
will ever be yours.

Only the rotten
and the abandoned
will fall before you:

the sinner and the wretch,
the violent and the afflicted.

Once blame is clear
you will enter in,

but you will no longer
seize just anyone.

You will be invoked

over mere croton sap,"
so they were told, all of Xibalba.

And so began the end
of their dominion,

as well as the ruin
of their reverence.

Their ancient day
was not glorious.

The ancient ones
fed only on strife.

Their ancient names
invoked no true gods.

The ugliness of their faces
evoked only fear.

They were strife-makers
and traitors.

They incited sin
and riotous violence.

They mastered deception
deep in their buried hearts,

both in lightness
and in darkness.

They were masters
of chaos and vexation,
or so they are called;

their faces remain hidden
down to the utter foundation.

Thus they lost their greatness
and their glory

and their rule was overthrown
by Hunahpu and Xbalanque.

° ° °

Now, at this same time,
their grandmother was keening and crying

before the ears of unripe maize
that had been planted in the hut.

They had sprouted,
but then dried and withered
when the twins were burned in the pit.

Then the ears of unripe maize
sprouted once again,

and their grandmother burned
copal incense in remembrance,

rejoicing in her heart,
that new life had returned.

So the twins were deified,
there, by their grandmother,

and she named the place:

> Center of the Home,
> Center of the Harvest,
>
> Living Maize,
> Bed of Earth.

She called it Center of the Home
and Center of the Harvest,

for it was at the very center,
there, inside the home,
that they planted the unripe maize.

She called it Bed of Earth
and Living Maize,

for it was level ground
where the unripe maize was planted

and the revived maize
had sent out living shoots again.
So Xmucane placed a name
on what Hunahpu and Xbalanque
had left planted behind them.

It was a way to remember them
by their grandmother.

    ° ° °

The first ones to die were their fathers,
a long time ago:

One Hunahpu and Seven Hunahpu.

They went to see him now,
face to face, there at Xibalba.

He spoke to them, their father,
now that Xibalba was defeated.

THE SUN, MOON, AND STARS

So they went to restore their father,
and Seven Hunahpu as well.

They went to honor them there,
at Devastation Ballcourt.

They simply wanted to see
his face made whole again,

so they asked him to name
everything: his mouth, his nose, his eyes.

His mouth could name itself
but then little more was said.

The skull could not speak
of its nose or its eyes.

But it had indeed spoken,
so they honored him with words.

They left their father's heart
there, at Devastation Ballcourt:

"You will be called upon, here,"
his sons said to him,
and his heart was comforted.

"You will be called upon first.
You will be worshiped by the children

born and bred in the light.
Your name will not be lost.

So be it," they said to their father,
when they comforted his heart.

"We have merely set things right
for your death, for your loss,

on account of the misfortune
and affliction done to you."

This was their counsel
when they had defeated Xibalba.
Then the twins rose together
as the central lights of the world.

They ascended straight into the sky:

        one arose as the sun,
        the other arose as the moon.

And the womb of the sky was filled
with light, and also the face of the earth.

They dwelled there, in the luminous sky,

and the four hundred boys
who died at the hands of Zipacna

rose up as their companions:
they climbed up into the sky
as constellations of stars.

Part Four

THE CREATION OF HUMANITY

This, then, is the beginning
of the conception of humans,

and the search for what would
become flesh for their bodies.

They spoke then, the ones called

> She who has borne children
> and He who has planted them,

> the Framer and the Shaper,
> Sovereign and Quetzal Serpent:

"Soon it will be dawn,
yet our work is not yet done.

There are not yet those
who will provide for this world,

and those who will sustain it:
children of light, born in the light.

Humanity must come
to people the face of the earth," they said,

and they gathered their thoughts
in the darkness of the night,

they searched and they sifted,
they pondered and wondered,

and their thoughts went out
into the world, bright and clear.

They found it. They discovered
what would serve as the flesh of humans.

This was only a little while
before the sun and moon and stars

would rise above the heads
of the Framer and the Shaper.

THE DISCOVERY OF MAIZE

It came from the cleft
of the mountain called Paxil,

it came from the pool
of bitter water called Cayala,

the yellow ears of maize,
the white ears of maize.

These, then, are the animals
that brought the food:

Fox and Coyote,
Parrot and Raven.

These four animals brought
word of the account

of the yellow ears of maize,
the white ears of maize.

They came from the cleft
of the mountain called Paxil,

and revealed the path
that led to the maize.

So the food was found,
that would grow into flesh

for these new people, framed
and shaped by their makers.

Water was their blood,
the blood of all humans.

She who has borne children
and He who has planted them

made the ripe ears of maize
enter into their flesh.

And so they all rejoiced
because it had been found,

such a wondrous mountain
crowded with richness,

thick with ripened ears
of yellow maize and white maize,

crowded as well with pataxte,
and crowded with cacao trees,

countless zapotes and anonas,
crowded with jocotes and nances,
as well as matasanos and honey.

All the sweetest foods fill
the citadel within that place

called Paxil and Cayala.
All the fruits, small and great,

all the planted fields, small and great,
the animals revealed the path.

Then the yellow ears of maize
and the white ears of maize,

were ground fine by Xmucane.
She ground them nine times,

and the food entered their flesh,
and water brought them strength,

and their arms began to fatten.
They grew thick and golden,

when they were made by the ones
called She who had borne chidren,

and He who has planted them,
by Sovereign and Quetzal Serpent.

So, our first mother and father
put their words into the world,

their framing and their shaping.
It was simply yellow ears of maize.

Ripened white ears of maize
became the flesh of humanity.

The arms and legs of our
first fathers were simply food.

They were four that were made,
and their flesh was merely food.

THE FIRST FOUR PEOPLE

These are the names of the first people
who were framed and shaped:

> The first person was Balam Quitze,
> or Jaguar Forest, as he is known.

> The second was Balam Acab,
> or Jaguar Night, as he is known.

> The third was Mahucutah,
> or Eminent Traveler, as he is known.

> The fourth was Iqui Balam,
> or Dark Wind Jaguar, as he is known.

These, then, are the names
of our first mothers and fathers.

THE VISION OF THE FIRST MEN

It is said these men were
simply framed and shaped:

they had no mother,
they had no father.

They were merely lone men.
No woman gave them birth.

Nor were they borne
by the Framer and the Shaper,

by She who has borne children,
and He who has planted them.

It was simply the pure spirit
and glinting spark of insight

of the Framer and the Shaper,
of Sovereign and Quetzal Serpent,

of She who has borne children,
and He who has planted them,

that framed and gave them shape.
They looked like true people,

and true people they became.
They spoke and they conversed.

They looked and they listened.
They walked and they grasped things,
and they held them in their hands.

They were excellent people,
well-made and handsome.

They appeared with manly faces
and began to breathe,
and so they became,

and they looked around them,
their vision coming all at once:

their sight was completed
by the world around them,

their knowledge was completed
by everything beneath the sky.

When they gazed about them,
they looked intently and deeply
into the womb of the sky and earth.

It took less than a moment to take it in.
In that brief time, they saw everything.

They had not yet taken a step,
when they already knew the world:

everything beneath the sky
was seen from where they looked,
and their knowledge was crowded full.

Their vision passed beyond the trees,
beyond the rocks and lakes and seas,
beyond the mountains and the valleys.

They were truly honored people,
Balam Quitze and Balam Acab,
Mahucutah and Iqui Balam.

GRATITUDE OF THE FIRST MEN

Then the four were asked
by the Framer and the Shaper:

"What is this, your being?

Can you feel it?
Do you know it?

Do you not look and listen?
Do you not speak and walk?

Look, then, and see
the roots of the sky.

Are the mountains not clear?
And the green valleys you see?

Try it, then," they were told.

So their vision of everything
rooted beneath the sky
was made complete,

and they gave thanks
to the Framer and Shaper:

"Truly, we thank you,
two times and three times,

that we were given form,
that we were given mouths,
that we were given faces,

so now we speak and we listen,
now we ponder and we move.

Well we know what we
learned and saw, far and near.

We saw the great and the small:
all there is in sky and earth.

So we give you thanks
that we were created,
that we were framed and shaped.

We took form because of you,
our grandmother and our grandfather,"

they said when they gave thanks
for their framing and their shaping.

Their knowledge of everything
they saw was perfect

as they looked into the four corners
and along the four sides
of everything within the sky and earth.

But this did not sound good
to the Framer and the Shaper.

"It's not good, what they said,
the ones that we have wrought:

      'We have learned everything,
      great and small,' they say."

THE DISPLEASURE OF THE GODS

So they took their knowledge back,

She who has borne children,
and He who has planted them.

"Now what will we do with them
so their vision merely reaches

nearby, so they will simply see
a little of the face of the earth?

It's not good what they say.
They were merely called

to be framed and shaped,
not to be mistaken for gods.

And yet if they do not multiply,
if they do not increase,

when shall it be sown?
When will dawn come?

If they do not prosper,
how can this come to be?

So we will simply undo them
a little. That is what is wanted,

because it is not good
what we discovered.

Their deeds could rival ours.
Their knowledge reaches far.
They could grasp everything."

So they spoke, Heart of Sky:

> Hurricane,
> Newborn Thunderbolt,
> and Sudden Lightning,
>
> Sovereign and Quetzal Serpent,
>
> She who has borne children,
> and He who has planted them,
>
> Xpiyacoc and Xmucane,
> the Framer and the Shaper, as they are called.

Then they remade the essence
of the people framed and shaped.

Their eyes were lightly clouded,
by Heart of Sky.

Like breath upon a mirror
or wind upon the water,
their eyes were veiled.

Their great vision was blunted.
Now they could only see nearby.

Things were only clear to them
right where they stood.

So their knowledge was lost,
the wisdom of those first four people.

It was lost there at its beginning,
at the very root of its planting.

This was the framing and the shaping
of our first grandfathers and fathers
by Heart of Sky and Heart of Earth.

THE FIRST FOUR WOMEN

Then their companions,
their wives, also came to be.

It was the gods alone
who conceived them.

As dreams come to sleepers,
they received them.

They were truly beautiful,
and now women stood beside

Balam Quitze and Balam Acab,
Mahucutah and Iqui Balam.

Now, with their wives
they truly came to life,

and soon their hearts rejoiced
because of their companions.

And these were the names
of each of the wives:

Cahapaluna, or Ocean Sky House,
        was the wife of Balam Quitze.

Chomiha, or Thick Shell House,
      was the wife of Balam Acab.

Tzununiha, or Hummingbird House,
      was the wife of Mahucutah.

Caquixaha, or Macaw House,
      was the wife of Iqui Balam.

These, then, are the names of their wives,
the ones who came to be our rulers.

They multiplied into nations,
both small and great.

This, then, is our root,
the root of the K'iche' people.

THE BEGINNINGS OF THE PEOPLE

There came to be many,
bloodletters and sacrificers.

There were no longer merely four,
but all of them sprang

from the four mothers
of we, the K'iche' people.

There were different names
for each of the peoples

that multiplied there,
where the sun comes up.

(Their names came to be:
      Tepew, or Sovereign,
      Oloman, or Place of Vital Fluid,
      K'ojaja, or Masker,
      K'enech Ajaw, or Sun Lord.

So they are called now,
the people that multiplied
in the place where the sun comes up.

The beginnings are known, then,
of the Tamub and Ilokab.

They came as one
from there in the East.

Balam Quitze was their grandfather,
the father of nine great houses
                              of Cavecs.

Balam Acab was their grandfather,
the father of nine great houses
                              of Nimhaibs.

Mahucutah was their grandfather,
the father of four great houses
                              of Ahau K'iche's.

Three divisions, three lines
of their existence.

Their names have not been lost:
the grandfathers and the fathers,

the ones who increased and flourished
in the land where the sun comes out.

The Tamub and the Ilocab came
along with the thirteen allied nations

of the thirteen houses:

        the Rabinal,
        the Cakchiquel,

Ah Tziquinahas,
the Zacahs and Lamacs,

the Cumatz,
the Tuhalahas,

the Uchabahas,
Ah Chumilahas,

Ah Quibahas,
As Batenahas,

the Acaul and Balamihas,
the Can Chahels,

and the Balam Colobs.

These are merely the great nations,
the ones of which we speak.

Many more came behind them,
each one a new division.

We shall not write their names,
only that they multiplied
there, where the sun comes out.)

Many people arrived
in those days of darkness,

there was not light
while they grew in number,

before the birth of the sun.
They moved as one people,

crowded together, wandering
aimlessly there in the East.

There was no one to provide,
no one to sustain them.

They merely lifted their faces
up to the sky, not knowing

where it was they wandered,
or where they wished to go.

They wandered the scrublands,
among black people and white people,

among people of many faces
who spoke many different tongues.

They wandered a long time,
uncertain and destitute,

there at the very foot of the sky,
there among the mountain people

with hidden faces and no homes,
who live in mountains great and small,
who are wayward and quarrelsome.

They looked there for the sunrise,
back when they had one tongue.

They did not yet call upon
gods in wood or stone.

They remembered the word
of their Framer and Shaper,
of Heart of Sky and Heart of Earth,
                              it is said.

It is said they offered pleas
            to be heartened,
            to let it be sown,
            to let the dawn come.

They were reverent,
people of esteemed words,
people of Honor and Respect.

They lifted their faces to the sky
as they pled for their daughters and sons:

            "O, you Framer,
            you Shaper,

look at us, hear us!
Do not abandon us.

Do not allow us
to be tossed aside.

You are the god
of both sky and earth,

the Heart of the Sky,
the Heart of the Earth.

Let our sign
and our word

live as long as the sun,
live as long as the light.

Then may it be sown.
Then the dawn can come.

Let there be green roads
and growing pathways.

Give us steady light,
so our nation is steady.

Give us favorable dawn,
so our nation is favored.

Give us the goodness of life,
so all creation prospers.

Give this to us, Hurricane,
Newborn Thunderbolt
and Sudden Lightning,

Newborn Nanavac,
Sudden Nanavac,
Falcon,
Hunahpu,

Sovereign,
Quetzal Serpent,

She who has borne children,
He who has planted them,
Xpiyacoc and Xmucane,

Grandmother of Day,
Grandmother of Light.

Then it will be sown.
Then the dawn can come," they said.

Then they fasted
and cried out in prayer.

They fixed their eyes
intently on the coming dawn.

They stared into the east.
They sought the Morning Star,

the Great Star that brings light
before the birth of the sun,

they gazed into the womb of the sky,
into the womb of the earth,

over the paths of the true people,
framed and shaped,

and then they spoke,   Balam Quitze,
                          Balam Acab,
                          Mahucutah,
                          Iqui Balam:

"Surely we await the dawn," they said.

THE FIRST DAWN

This, then, is the dawn,
the coming of the sun,
as well as the moon and stars.

Their joy was wondrous,

> Balam Quitze,
> Balam Acab,
> Mahucutah,
> Iqui Balam,

when they saw the Morning Star.

It came out first,
brilliant face gleaming,

and they unwrapped their copal incense,
for the sun would soon be there.

Triumph swelled their hearts
as they unfolded the leaves.

There were three kinds of incense
to lift up their heartfelt thanks:

> Mixtam Incense was the name
> of what Balam Quitze carried.

Cavistan Incense was the name
of what Balam Acab carried.

Divine Incense was the name
of what Mahucutah carried.

These three copal incenses
were what they burned,

as they sent out smoke
to meet the coming sun.

They wept bitter tears
as they waved the smoke,

as they shook the precious copal,
the burning, sacred copal.

They wept for they
had never seen the sun,
never witnessed its birth.

Then the sun came up,
and all the animals rejoiced,

the great ones and small ones,
coming up from the river,

and out from the canyons,
waiting on the mountaintops,

their faces turned as one
toward the brilliant sunlight,

and the jaguars and the pumas
broke out roaring

and the parrot cried out,
the first of the birds,

and all the animals rejoiced,
the great birds and the small ones,

and the eagle and the white vulture
lifted their wings in the light.

However many nations
live in the world today,

however many countless people,
they all had but one dawn.

And then the face of the earth
was dried by the sun.

The sun was like a person
when he first revealed himself.

His face glowed hot,
and so he dried the earth.

Before his coming,
the earth was wet.

The face of the earth was soggy
before he showed himself.

He only ascended upward.
He was just like a person,
and his heat was unbearable.

He revealed his true self
only when he was born.

What remains now
is merely a reflection.

"The sun we see now
 is not the real one,"
              they say in the old accounts.

∘ ∘ ∘

Joy filled the hearts
of Balam Quitze and Balam Acab.

It filled the hearts
of Mahucutah and Iqui Balam.

They rejoiced in wonder
when it dawned.

There were not many people then.
There were only a few there,
on the mountaintop, called Hacavitz.

It was there that they dawned.

And there that they burned
and waved the smoke of their copal
toward the coming of the sun.

This was their mountain,
this was their plain.

This is where they came,
Balam Quitze and Balam Acab,
Mahucutah and Iqui Balam, as they are called.

They multiplied there,
on the mountaintop
that would become their citadel.

It was there that the sun,
and the moon and the stars
first made their light.

Everything on the earth
and under the sky
glowed with the dawn
and became clear.

Notes

INTRODUCTION

vii *"it was with great reserve"* Francisco Ximénez, *Historia de la provincia de San Vicente de Chiapa y Guatemala* [1722], Biblioteca "Goathemala"de la Sociedad de Georgrafia e Historia de Guatemala Publication I, I.i.5, Guatemala Tipografia Nacional.

vii *"superstition and the lies"* The full quote is as follows: "We found a large number of books of these characters and, as they contained nothing in which there were not to be seen superstition and lies of the devil, we burned them all, which they regretted to an amazing degree and caused them much affliction." Fr. Diego de Landa, *Relación de las cosas de Yucatán [1566]*, trans. A. M. Tozzer [1941], Peabody Museum Papers, vol. 18, Peabody Museum of American Archaeology and Ethnology, Cambridge, Massachusetts.

ix *"It was like finding"* Chip Brown, "El Mirador, the Lost City of the Maya," *Smithsonian*, May 2011, https://www.smithsonianmag.com/history/el-mirador-the-lost-city-of-the-maya-1741461/.

ix *"to find this story"* Ibid.

x   *"When the words"* Allen Christenson, *Popol Vuh: The Sacred Book of the Maya* (Norman: University of Oklahoma Press, 2007), 17.

xi   *"the way in which clouds"* Fr. Domingo de Basseta, *Vocabulario en lengua quiché* [1968], typescript by William Gates of the original in the Bibliothèque Nationale, Paris [1921], W. E. Gates Collection, Special Collections and Manuscript Archives, Harold B. Lee Library, Brigham Young University.

The Popol Vuh: A Reader's Companion

Part One

The Preamble of the *Popol Vuh* begins with a resonant pronouncement: "The root of the ancient word starts here." The life of the text springs from its *xe'*, where its roots enter the earth, and the story unfurls organically from this point, fed by the living tendrils of its language. Our unknown scribes frame this telling as the echo of a divine act, evoking the gods who "spoke the world into being / with luminous words and clear truth." The acts of writing and planting are twinned here: just as the seed is planted within the four corners of the maize field, so these words are planted within the four sides of the page. The making of the world and the making of the book merge, and we are reminded that this telling is an echo of a more ancient book, "that way of seeing clearly that came from beside the sea, / that account of our origins in the shadows, / that place where we see the dawn of life, as it is said."

Yet a hint of darkness hovers at the edge of these proceedings: the need to set this story down "amidst talk of God / under the rule of Christendom" before it disappears back into the shadows, now that those who read the ancient book have hidden their faces. One can envision the K'iche' priests consulting this ancient text, gathered on their four-cornered council mat, itself an embodiment of the Maya conception of the four-cornered universe. Thus maize field, council mat, page, and universe are all invoked, their four sides and corners measured and staked, merging into a single space of gathering and sustenance.

Then the first words of creation arrive: "Here we are."

The imminent dawn of life unfolds before us, and it is one

of the wonders of the *Popol Vuh* that we are present to gaze upon it. The K'iche' equivalent of the present tense brings with it a compelling immediacy. An effect, I think, that is hard to overstate. Imagine if the first book of Genesis employed such a technique: *Here we are. All is without form. All is void. The breath of God is hovering across the face of the waters. Then God says, Let there be light. And look! there is light, and the light is good.* The sense of drama is palpable. The ancient authors of the Popol Vuh then draw us even further into the moment, as the opening lines insist: "*These* are the first words. / *This* is the first speaking." The telling of this tale overlaps with the ancient words it contains, and the narrative thread pulls snug, drawing two points of time together into a single stitch, the eternal *now* of the story.

🝆

Dualities abound in the *Popol Vuh.* The epic is not the story of a hero, but hero twins. And we do not encounter a lone omnipotent god speaking the world into existence, but a framer and a shaper, each containing multiplicities within, and themselves echoes of a grandfather and a grandmother, Xpiyacoc and Xmucane. (One can imagine the early audience of the Spaniards accepting the mystery of the Trinity without blinking an eye, considering the "three in one" conception of Heart of Sky contained in the manuscript.) So it is perhaps natural that the creation of this world stems from an ongoing conversation, a collaboration where the gods question and hearten one another, "braiding together their words and their thoughts" to form new life. This is conception in both senses of the word, as thoughts spring into being.

The silence of the world is a waiting silence, a suspended silence. Everything is contained in its nothingness. The land is called from the sea, and the mountains are called from the land. These elements are not so much created as released, unfurling with a force of their own. The making of the world is a puzzle to be unlocked, a flow to be undammed. "Let it be uncovered. Let it be found / how we will frame . . ." The passive verb constructions grant agency to the world, not its makers. These gods ponder and wonder, resembling artists in the way they listen to their medium.

Clearly, this is a conversation intended to be continued: the gods yearn to hear their names spoken back to them. They wish to be called upon, to be remembered. Such acknowledgment is the only way to be made whole, and to persist through time. Yet the power of language has its limits. Mountains, rivers, and all the creatures of the world might appear as quickly as they are summoned. But humans are another matter.

After creating the animals, the gods instruct: "It's time to speak to one another now." They are greeted with chitters, roars, and squawks, and though the gods make a point to give them all homes, their inability to speak intelligently condemns them to living in a cycle of eating and being eaten, with no prospect for transcendence via the word. So the gods turn to the task of making humanity, and the first person is molded from mud. But this is not the clay of Adam. Misshapen, neckless, and soggy as overcooked vegetables, the being is immediately dismissed as a mistake and allowed to melt back into the earth. This is the roughest of rough drafts. The next attempt reaches a bit further out of the earth: men are carved from wood, women woven from reeds. And though these creatures could chatter and walk,

Their hearts were blank, their minds empty.
They held no memory of who had made them.

So once again, they are cast away and destroyed: the gods summon a flood. Yet whereas the figure of mud is allowed to simply dwindle, these figures of wood are savaged. Their shortcoming is clear: they lack *na'wik*, the capacity to notice, understand, and perceive. They lived as mindless creatures of appetite, who took and did not give, and thus we see this empty consumption come full circle in the ravages of the flood, as they are literally consumed by what fed them: their meat, their corn, their cooking pots and fires. To be thoughtless is to be inhuman, a mere monkey; such people will not do.

Part Two

After the flood is unleashed, the poem unmoors itself in time, circling back to the era before the watery destruction, when the world was still peopled with these wooden dummies who weren't true people. The true sun has not yet dawned, and, fittingly, these false and thoughtless figures of wood look to a false and thoughtless god, called Seven Macaw.

Seven Macaw and his two sons, Zipacna and Cabracan, form a sort of blowhard trinity, a callow family of pretenders in need of disposal so that the true day might dawn. They are not without powers of their own: Seven Macaw soars above the treetops, and one son possesses hulking strength while the other causes earthquakes. But their vision is limited. It does "not touch / everything beneath the face of the sky," and they live in a dim world of predawn light, mistaking the shimmer of gold for that of the sun. Like the figures carved from wood, they are lacking in *na'wik* and incapable of seeing the truth, even when it unwittingly tumbles from their own mouths. Their words are empty even to themselves.

And so the hero twins, Hunahpu and Xbalanque, stroll into the poem. They arrive out of nowhere and out of need, an entrance that is both casual and necessary, shouldering their blowguns to take aim at this pride that has puffed itself up into evil. The boys present themselves as wandering orphans, with no names and no origins, in perfect antithesis to the hollow bravado of Seven Macaw and his clan. They will be our protagonists for the next hundred pages, ultimately grappling with death itself to prepare the world for the dawn of the first day. Yet these boys are still boys, both puckish and cunning. When direct confrontation with Seven Macaw results in Hunahpu's arm being ripped from its socket (and then hung on a hook above the hearth fire, in a gruesome and uncanny echo of Grendel's dismembered limb in *Beowulf*), they resort to their wiles and deliver comeuppances via a series of playful, if fatal, pranks.

Seven Macaw's appetite for wealth is clear; precious stones are literally embedded into his teeth. When the boys engage in their rudimentary dental work to "heal" him, they pluck out the jewels and insist upon filling the cavities with ground white corn. It is a fitting moment—the gleam of Seven Macaw's false wealth has been removed and replaced with stuff of actual sustenance. His son's fates are equally fitting: Zipacna boasts that he made the mountains, yet ultimately the mountains make him. After being duped into entering a cave (in a parody of the sex act), he is crushed by a collapsing tonnage of rock and turned to stone. And Cabracan's yen for shaking the earth is undone when the boys use his craving for flesh to trick him into swallowing a bit of dirt; the earth becomes a part of him and his strength vanishes.

Unlike conflicts to come, there is not any sense these adversaries pose a grave threat—after all, the boys can shoot down birds using only "bolts of air" and conjure a scuttling crab from stones. The story even briefly interrupts itself when Hunahpu loses his arm, to assure the reader that "the first round was not the full battle." We are thus freed to revel in the section's playful comic touches, such as when the loudmouth Seven Macaw cradles his broken jaw and announces: "My mouth is the source of all my agony!" The moment is slyly perfect: the downfall of all three pretenders is caused by the overactive flapping of their own jaws—too much boasting, too much appetite, too much hungering—in short, too much too much-ness.

Part Three

Once Hunahpu and Xabalanque have sprung onto the page, "two boys / who'd done the word of Heart of Sky," we circle back in time again, tracing their thread further back to its origins. We begin with the father of the hero twins, One Hunahpu, and his brother and companion, Seven Hunahpu, described as One Hunahpu's "second self." Seven Hunahpu is the moon to One Hunahpu's sun, offering an unmistakable antecedent to the symbiotic kinship of Hunahpu and Xbalanque. They are always together, with Hunahpu leading the way. Such an arrangement offers the balance and equilibrium of twinship with the stability of a clear hierarchy. There is no doubt as to who generates the light and who reflects it.

One and Seven Hunahpu spend the length of their days throwing dice and playing ball. At first glance, this may not seem particularly industrious, yet they are visionaries who hold a divine spark, and in both pursuits they engage the unseen movements of fate and the cosmos. Their ball-playing serves as the catalyst for their encounter with mortality, disturbing the Lords of Death with the steady pulse it beats onto the roof of the underworld. It is both a game and not a game at all.

This resonates with what we know of ball-playing among the K'iche'. Ball courts held prominent positions in the citadels of the K'iche', nestled among their temples and tombs. As with all games, the sport operated within its set of fixed and seemingly arbitrary rules and codes—and though not all of these rules are known today, it is clear that one was not to touch the ball with either hands or feet, and the ball was not to touch the ground. The players strapped on arm and leg bracers and broad leather belts with wooden yokes, thrusting hips and thighs to keep the ball in the air. In this way, the ball embodied the sun, a cosmic sphere that had to be kept eternally moving, held aloft by the dance of the game. As long as the game persisted, the players inhabited a divine space. Without their movements, time itself would cease.

The ball was made of the sap of the rubber tree and, being solid, was remarkably heavy. I've held a facsimile in my hands, roughly eight pounds of solid rubber—easily capable of delivering serious injury, breaking bones, even knocking one senseless. This ball bore the same name as what composed it, the rubber sap or *kik'*, the word the K'iche' use for any vital fluid, be it the fluid coursing through a tree or the blood in the veins. This merging of vital fluid and cosmic sphere, of blood and sun, generates tremendous metaphoric possibility within the text, particularly when one's opponent in the ball game is death itself.

Because it is, in essence, the vitality of One and Seven Hunahpu that draws the ire of the Lords of Death: it is their stomping, their shouting, the steady pulse of the bouncing ball with its echo of a beating heart. In the scene where they bid their tearful grandmother good-bye, they acknowledge that they have no choice once they have been summoned to Xibalba. One cannot turn down a date with death, after all. Yet as they rush off to play their game, they leave a bit of themselves tucked safely at home:

"But we'll leave our rubber ball behind."

*Then they climbed and tied it
snug under the roof of their hut.*

"You'll hear its steady beat again—
we will play once we've returned."

Their promise resonates with an innocence that seems almost
willful, as well as the poignancy of any good-bye where one
suspects one might not return. One and Seven Hunahpu are
leaving their essence behind, hidden snugly into the roof over
their heads, and though their own hearts will soon stop beat-
ing forever, their *kik'* will return in the form of another, and
Xmucane will indeed hear its steady pulse once again.

An air of foreboding hangs over this journey from its very out-
set, and once One and Seven Hunahpu have chosen the black
road at the crossroads, the western road that leads to the setting
sun, their fate is a foregone conclusion. Their *na'wik* seems to fail
them as they mistake wooden figures for gods, becoming a sub-
ject of ridicule to the Lords of Death. The many trials of Xibalba
are previewed, but One and Seven Hunahpu do not even get
past the first: the riddling task brought to them in the House
of Darkness, which demands they bring back their torches and
cigars both used and unconsumed. Such a feat would demand a
spark that does not consume itself, a fire that does not destroy
what it feeds upon—in short, the spark of life itself.

After the two are summarily sacrificed, their bodies are bur-
ied at the ball court, and One Hunahpu's head is slung into the
branches of the calabash tree. A glimmer of One Hunahpu's
divine essence seems to return upon his death, however, as his
head infuses the calabash tree with a strange and sudden fertil-
ity. The tree promptly bears fruit for the very first time, and the

lords of Xibalba come out to marvel, sensing greatness. They declare that no one shall cut the fruit of the tree nor enter the shade below it, and so "all the Xibalbans confined themselves." Thus One Hunahpu succeeds in death where he failed in life: he creates an inviolate place of vitality in the underworld, an endlessly fruitful branch that cannot be consumed, setting the stage for one of the most remarkable scenes in the *Popol Vuh*, the encounter between Lady Blood and the Tree of One Hunahpu.

※

The story of Lady Blood strikes a chord that is at once both profoundly archetypal and utterly strange. It contains strong echoes of the Eve myth with its forbidden fruit motif, as well as moments that evoke the immaculate conception, with the miraculous begetting of the hero twins and Lady Blood's maidenly insistence upon her virginity when confronted by her father. (Her protestations ring true, because they are—she has never known "the face of any man," only a skull.) There is even an echo of Snow White, who also had to offer up a counterfeit heart to feed the cannibal appetites of her tormentor and confirm her "death." But unlike Eve's encounter with her forbidden tree, Lady Blood's intrepid will asserts itself out in the open—her own burgeoning fertility seems to recognize itself in the tree, and she asserts "I will not die. / I will not be lost." There is no pretext of being duped. On the contrary, when One Hunahpu confronts her, asking what she could possibly desire from arid bone, she owns up to her hungering curiosity, insisting "But I do desire it."

So she reaches her hand up into the branches, where One Hunahpu's skull spits into it, and in this moment, the hero twins are conceived, their mother a Lady of the underworld, their grandfather a Lord of Death. In this marriage of life and death, a curious inversion occurs: life speaks through the jaws of a skull while death takes the form of a fertile young woman. The act seems to transcend standard notions of morality as well. Later, when Lady Blood is begging for her life from the owls, she asserts that "what grows within me / does not come from fornication. // It was an act of mere creation." In listening to her desire, Lady Blood becomes the virgin mother of young gods, and life springs from the husk of its antecedent, its desiccated seed.

It is no wonder, then, that upon coming to the face of the earth and entering the household of Xmucane, she passes the test of the maize field with such ease, netting her miraculous harvest. She brings with her the otherworldly fertility of the Tree of One Hunahpu, telling Xmucane that she will "look upon his face again" in the ones that she is carrying. It seems that One and Seven Hunahpu are not dead, but rather germinating. In this cycling dance of energy, it is not the individual self that matters so much as the spark of vitality itself, persisting through time. Nothing is lost if the line continues.

❀

But it is imperative that the line *does* continue. And in the tale of One Batz and One Chouen we encounter the consequences of what happens when this vitality is stopped from flowing from one generation to the next, when the "brilliance is blocked."

It is clear that before the birth of the hero twins, One Batz and One Chouen were exemplary sons. They honor their origins, see the world clearly, and carry the "ingenious spark" within them as they stand in the place of their father, One Hunahpu. But the birth of the twins infects them with envy, and the affliction seems to clog the flow of their good nature. Hunahpu and Xbalanque are cast out into the wild to die, but they sleep contentedly on simmering anthills and nestle comfortably into thorn bushes instead. They are clearly at home in this world.

When One Batz and One Chouen devour more than their fair share, commandeering the game the twins have shot, the boys respond with an equanimity that is almost zen. They "knew their own clear natures" and they use this light to see. Their power is rooted in a self-knowledge that recognizes the divine spark within. One Batz and One Chouen, on the other hand, have "lost themselves" and ultimately serve as the source of their own demise. The hero twins do not so much defeat the brothers as function as a mirror of their distorted longings. When the brothers follow their appetites into the treetops, they are confronted with their desire for ascendancy, as the trees begin to swell and shoot skyward. They are soon begging to be brought low, and by story's end, they have devolved from their godly status into monkeys, suffering the same fate as the figures of wood. They are laughable, even to their own grandmother.

❁

The hero twins assume their just place in Xmucane's house and prove to be gifted but indifferent farmers. Coaxing fertility from the world presents little challenge to the sons of Lady Blood, but they would rather go hunting in the mountains. Yet when they hear that One Hunahpu's rubber ball, his *kik'*, is tucked up under the roof of their grandmother's hut, their hearts leap. It is a moment of wonderful symmetry: the sons' hearts beat at the discovery of their father's blood.

The *Popol Vuh* is built resolutely upon such symmetries, continually folding back into itself, like a fractal or a repeatedly halved piece of paper. The story teems with doubles and echoes: its world is created through one god constantly mirroring back the intent of another. Not only are its heroes twinned, but one pair of brothers must supplant another in order to claim their due in their own household, and the twins themselves provide an uncanny echo of their fathers. This focus on duality is embodied in Mayan script itself, written in double columns, the glyphs placed side by side, as if in conversation with one another. The structure of the central section of the myth functions in the same way. The story is essentially told twice—Hunahpu and Xbalanque discover the gaming things, they disturb the lords of Xibalba with their raucous ball-playing, and soon the owls arrive with the summons, and we sense ourselves being drawn down the rabbit hole once again.

Upon receiving the summons, Xmucane recognizes the echo, noting the messengers are "just like those . . . that came before / when their father / went off to die." Her character may be a part of the weave, but she nonetheless recognizes the greater pattern. She sends the twins news via the louse, and in the ensuing fable we witness what happens to her urge to swallow an unpleasant truth, as it is eaten deeper and deeper into a succession of animal bellies: louse enters toad enters snake enters falcon. But the painful truth will out—and in fact, this truth accelerates, as each time it is swallowed, it moves up the food chain, traveling only more quickly to its destination, finally arriving on the wings of a falcon. The vigor with which the twins try to extricate the message suggests a buried desire: this is a journey that, on some level, they wish to undertake.

The descent into Xibalba is a familiar one. We have, after all, been down this road before. The twins are returning to the home of their mother and grandfather, their lives functioning as the thread that stitches the realm aboveground to the realm below. They cross the same rivers, encounter the same crossroads. But this is not simple repetition. It is one of the most necessary stages for anyone wishing to author their own fate: it is a chance for revision.

So the boys walk into the same story-structure as their fathers, but they bring with them an inner vision their fathers lacked. It is a remarkably pleasing narrative device, as if the boys possess *l'esprit d'escalier*, the wit of the staircase, as when one discovers the perfect comeback only after leaving a party. The mosquito they send as an advance scout embodies this foresight, gathering the names of the Lords of Death and the seating chart in the great hall of Xibalba so that once the twins arrive, they may engage the lords on equal footing.

The same jokes are attempted—the wooden dummies, the scorching bench that serves as the proverbial hot seat—but the twins dismiss them with clear eyes and summon each lord by name. To call someone by proper name is a sign of both honor and respect—it forms the root of the proper relationship between humanity and the gods—but it is also a way to define, or even confine, a person within that identity. When asked about their origins, the boys playfully reply: "We must have come from somewhere / but we don't know where that is?" There is a philosophical truth beneath the joke—who can ever fully know their own origins—and by remaining nameless, the boys stay elusive and ungraspable, setting the table for some delicious dramatic irony, as the Xibalban lords—the twins' grandfather among them—wonder aloud about their lineage: "Where did these two come from? Who was the one who bore these children?"

When the trials of Xibalba begin, the boys' fraternity with the natural world serves them well. When faced with the test that undid their father, One Hunahpu, the twins tuck fireflies into the tips of their cigars and use the shimmering tail feather of a macaw to impersonate the torch. Nature readily provides them with a spark that does not consume itself. Ants help them gather the bowls of petals after they lose the first ball game, they offer bones to the jaguars, and they weather both extreme heat and extreme cold without batting an eyelash. Hunahpu does not die even when he is decapitated by the razor-slash of a death-bat. Xbalanque merely asks the animal kingdom to gather its food—what sustains each of them—and Hunahpu's lost head is replaced with a cleverly carved squash. Once the twins retrieve the head by duping the Xibalban lords, it is "planted" back onto the vine of his neck, to no apparent ill effect. In this final act of revision, skull and squash become interchangeable; we have circled all the way back to the calabash tree of One Hunahpu and effectively undone the indignities he suffered so long ago.

🐚

Once the boys have taken everything the lords of Xibalba can muster and triumphed, their hearts are visited by a sign: the time of death is now at hand. It is an intriguing moment: now that the twins have transcended death, it can be embraced. Or as they put it, with their deceptive simplicity: "How can we not die forever?" So after making it clear that they are not deceived by the attempt to trap them in the roasting pit, the boys join hands and dive headfirst into the fire. There is something wildly liberating in the action. One cannot defeat a thing by avoiding it—and the twins remain united and vital even in death, clasping their hands together as they make the choice to plunge in headlong.

And why not? Life springs eternally from death in the story, and here that persistence is linked explicitly to togetherness and language. There is great emphasis throughout the Popol Vuh on paying homage to powerful words by repeating them with accuracy. When the gods instruct the animals on how to pray, they literally attempt to put words in their mouths—"Say it like this"—and each summons to Xibalba is accompanied by the reminder that "the owls repeated every word . . . every word is what they spoke." In secretly summoning Xulu and Paqam before they die, the boys continue this pattern; by providing direction on what to say after their death, they insert themselves as narrators of their own story, with the ability to speak from beyond the grave.

The twins have instructed Xulu and Paqam to grind their bones to a fine white powder and mix it with water, and the directions are followed to the letter. The recipe foreshadows the making of the first true people out of maize and water, knowledge that would have been a given among the Maya. The boys may be gods, but they are also, in a sense, the first true humans, as they spring back to life from finely ground meal and water. The moment also serves as it a gentle reminder that our narrative spiral back in time is now nearly complete: the boys are on the cusp of setting the stage for the earth to be peopled and the first day to dawn.

So, for the third and final time, the boys walk into the story as unknowns, nameless orphans with no clear origin—just as in their first encounter with Seven Macaw. As dancers, they now exist almost outside of language, primarily using their bodies to speak, and they transfix the lords of Xibalba with their marvelous powers of resurrection. Their performance is both sly and masterful, whetting the appetite of the lords until they are crazed with hunger yet also displaying the clear truth of the twins' intent: they are bringing resurrection to the underworld, as readily as green grass springs from a brown and withered root.

When Xbalanque goes so far as to lop off the head of Hunahpu, reenacting their recent escapade on the ball court, the lords still do not recognize who stands revived before them. They beg to be killed next and, not surprisingly, receive their wish. So death itself is killed, and from this point forward, its dominion is no longer absolute—it will feed only upon the "rotten and the abandoned," the "already spent" and "already spilled," the "brittle and easily broken." At this moment, Hunahpu and Xbalanque finally reveal their names in Xibalba, placing their signature on their finest work. Fittingly, this is when the stalk of withered corn in Xmucane's hut sprouts a green shoot: once generative life has found a home underground.

In the wake of their victory, the twins visit the calabash tree of One Hunahpu and encounter their father for the very first time. They wish to see him made whole, and in an attempt to revive him, they ask his head to name the senses it once used to engage the world: its mouth, its nose, its eyes. This faith in the power of language is touching, as is the image of the hopeful boys, who, in spite of vanquishing death itself, still look to their father to set things right. The skull opens its mouth to speak, but "little more was said." There is a suspended moment where we sense the twins waiting, just as we waited in the hush before the gods spoke the world into existence. But the skull does not speak of its hollow nose, its empty stare. It cannot. Mortal vision does not reach beyond the horizon of death. Death's dominion may no longer by absolute, but the grasp of our sense will end. It is, quite literally, a breathtaking moment, offering a note of quiet emptiness in the midst of exultation.

With the wrongs against their father rectified, and an assurance that his name will be remembered, the twins ascend into the sky: Hunahpu as the sun, Xbalanque as the moon. Our story, which began when "light / just dimmed the air with early dawn," has taken place in the hinterlands of time and is now on the verge of entering the calendar. We may see the defeat of Seven Macaw as foreshadowing the duping of the Xibalban lords, or we may, in that moment, be hearing the echo well before we encounter the source of the sound. The *Popol Vuh* makes no attempt to order all of these events into a perfectly linear progression. The story sense works, and that is enough. Once Hunahpu and Xbalanque achieve their apotheosis, the celestial bodies that mark the months, days, and years are in place: the calendric wheels can begin to turn and time as we measure it can commence. It is up to the ball-playing twins to keep the spheres aloft forever—or at least until time draws to a close.

Part Four

So we have returned to the beginning: the world has been washed clean by the flood, the false gods removed, the prospect of revival planted firmly underground. We are finally ready to finish what's been started: creating human beings who can see the world clearly and speak intelligently and gratefully of whence they came. The ingredients the gods use for this version are simple but effective. "The food was found / that would grow into flesh"—maize and water. This is the fourth draft, and it works. After animals proved unsatisfactory, the gods drafted people from mud, from wood and reeds, and, finally, from corn. An implied narrative lives within this progression: life is drawn from the dirt up through the stalk toward the sunlight where, with a little water, the fruit of the plant finally blossoms. It is not until mud and branch have reached toward the sky that growth is complete. Everything looks to the sun.

Four people are created, one for each corner of the sky, each side of the cosmos, each point on the compass. These are the "mother-fathers" of their respective K'iche' lineages, and they are the true people the gods have wished: "They spoke and they conversed. / They looked and they listened. / They walked and they grasped things, / and they held them in their hands." Their vision is vast from the first moment of consciousness, beginning with a state akin to nirvana, as they take in the entire world in a transcendent glance: "They saw everything." It is an interpenetrating sort of vision: their sight is "completed / by the world around them" and "their knowledge was completed / by everything beneath the sky." Clearly, the reach of their *na'wik* does not exceed its grasp, and they express the fullness of their gratitude with simple elegance.

It is a marvelous beginning for humanity. A little too good, perhaps. The gods are troubled. These creatures were "not to be mistaken for gods," and thus the decision is made to "undo them / a little." It is a curious moment, as this version of people seems to meet the hopes of the gods so completely. There is more than a hint of threat and jealousy in their words, yet there may be other energies at play, as it is also at this moment that the gods wonder aloud if such transcendent creatures might "not multiply" and "if they do not increase / when shall it be sown? / When will dawn come?" Perhaps if the vision of these people is limited, they will be driven by their incompletion to yearn more deeply for one another. So their eyes are "lightly clouded" by Heart of Sky, imbuing the creation of humanity with both the glimmer of transcendence and the pang of loss.

Four women are made for the first four men, each of their names containing the root for "house." The women are equated with structure, shelter, and the people begin to quickly multiply in those "days of darkness . . . before the birth of the sun." Crowds of people wander aimlessly in this land of eternal dusk, not knowing where they are or where they wish to go. They have no signpost, wandering the scrublands "among black people and white people." They are moving outside the boundaries of time, and it is hard not to hear echoes of a collective memory of human migration here, stemming back across the Bering land bridge into a murky prehistory of nomadic wandering. They need "steady light" so their "nation will be steady" and they gather to wait, staring intently toward the east. When the sun first breaks the horizon, it is greeted with a joyous symphony of cries. The arrival of the first sunrise is the arrival of a new beginning. Of days that can be measured and counted. Of signs by which to plant and harvest. Of history and culture. Of a way to grasp and hold the world.

Leslie Bazzett

MICHAEL BAZZETT is the author of *The Interrogation; You Must Remember This*, which received the 2014 Lindquist & Vennum Prize for Poetry; *Our Lands Are Not So Different;* and a chapbook, *The Imaginary City*. His poems have appeared in numerous publications, including *Ploughshares, The Sun, Massachusetts Review, Pleiades*, and *Best New Poets*. A longtime faculty member at The Blake School, Bazzett has received the Bechtel Prize from Teachers & Writers Collaborative and is a 2017 National Endowment for the Arts Fellow. He lives in Minneapolis.

milkweed
editions

Founded as a nonprofit organization in 1980,
Milkweed Editions is an independent publisher. Our mission
is to identify, nurture and publish transformative literature,
and build an engaged community around it.

Milkweed Editions is based in Bdé Óta Othúŋwe
(Minneapolis) within Mní Sota Makhóčhe, the traditional
homeland of the Dakhóta people. Residing here since time
immemorial, Dakhóta people still call Mní Sota Makhóčhe
home, with four federally recognized Dakhóta nations and
many more Dakhóta people residing in what is now the state
of Minnesota. Due to continued legacies of colonization,
genocide, and forced removal, generations of Dakhóta people
remain disenfranchised from their traditional homeland.
Presently, Mní Sota Makhóčhe has become a refuge and
home for many Indigenous nations and peoples, including
seven federally recognized Ojibwe nations. We humbly
encourage our readers to reflect upon the historical legacies
held in the lands they occupy.

ABOUT SEEDBANK

Just as repositories around the world gather seeds in an effort
to ensure biodiversity in the future, Seedbank gathers works
of literature from around the world that foster reflection on
the relationship of human beings with place and
the natural world.

milkweed.org

We are aided in our mission by generous individuals
who make a gift to underwrite books on our list. Special
underwriting for *The Popol Vuh* was provided by
the following supporters:

Keith and Mary Bednarowski

Christopher and Katherine Crosby

The Hlavka Family

Bill and Cheryl Hogle

Hart and Susie Kuller

Interior design by Mary Austin Speaker
Typeset in Caslon

Adobe Caslon Pro was created by Carol Twombly
for Adobe Systems in 1990. Her design was inspired by
the family of typefaces cut by the celebrated engraver
William Caslon I, whose family foundry served
England with clean, elegant type from the early
Enlightenment through the turn of the
twentieth century.